FEMINAISSANCE

♭
LES FIGUES PRESS
Los Angeles

FEMINAISSANCE
FIRST EDITION

Edited by Christine Wertheim
Editor's Entries & Selection ©2010, Christine Wertheim
All works printed with the permission of the authors.
Authors retain copyrights to individual pieces.

Printed in Michigan
Design by Teresa Carmody

ISBN 10: 1-934254-17-7
ISBN 13: 978-1-934254-17-2
Library of Congress Control Number: 2009933957

Distributed by SPD / Small Press Distribution
1341 Seventh Street
Berkeley, CA 94710
www.spdbooks.org

ƒ
Les Figues Press
Post Office Box 7736
Los Angeles, CA 90007
323.734.4732 / info@lesfigues.com
www.lesfigues.com
www.lesfigues.blogspot.com

Contents

Publishers' and Editor's Foreword
Carmody, Place, and Wertheim
ix

Introduction:
Essentialism: To Be or Not to Be
Christine Wertheim
xi

Numbers Trouble
Juliana Spahr and Stephanie Young
3

The Feminist Writers' Guild
Dodie Bellamy
3

"Say Did You See that Wind from the East":
a feminist is
Susan McCabe
3

Striving to Be a Man: Gender-Altering
Forces in Post-Feminist America
Wanda Coleman
21

Continuity
Chris Kraus
23

Embracing Form:
Pedagogical Sketches of Black Women
Students Influenced by Hip Hop
Tracie Morris
37

In Praise of the Anti-Social
Maggie Nelson
37

from *Incubation: a space for monsters*
Bhanu Kapil
14

tapestry
Eileen Myles
14

Two Poems
Tracie Morris
20

Gender Trouble
Juliana Spahr
28

from *Red Parts*
Maggie Nelson
28

Chapter Seven, or,
I Do What I Don't Want To Do
Stephanie Young
45

Four Poems
Susan McCabe
52

Daguerreotype of a Girl
Lidia Yuknavitch
70

The First Gurgitation is a Sentence
Vanessa Place & Carolyn K. Place
75

RAPE
Wanda Coleman
90

Points of Pressure
Caroline Bergvall
58

The Laughing Medusa
Meiling Cheng
59

Figuring the Imaginary: Writing into the Strange Genitalia, or Notes Towards a Fabular Irradiated Accelerate Social Imaginary
Bhanu Kapil
79

Somagraph
Meiling Cheng
88

What Is Gender Today?
Eileen Myles
104

I Am Madam
Vanessa Place
108

Unreliable Witness
Chris Kraus
96

Sexspace
Dodie Bellamy
100

from **Shorter Chaucer Tales, 2006**
Caroline Bergvall
111

mOUther pOEmes
Christine Wertheim
119

from *psalm*
Lidia Yuknavitch
2
20
36
58
78

Contributors' Notes
126

Acknowledgments
129

Dedication
Christine Wertheim

Another anthology of women's writing!

Don't we live in a post-gendered, post-subjective age where isolating the work of specifically defined groups is outmoded? Aren't revolutions obsolete in our new world order where the subject of power has been emptied? Leaving nothing to fight over? Isn't this what postmodernism taught us?

Perhaps grand revolutions are passé. But "tiny revolts" are necessary (see Dodie Bellamy's piece inside).

Sexuality may be freer, and women may play seriously in all spheres, but for all practical purposes most western games still rely on the founding myth of patriarchy—that the One/Ideal/Time/Law/Truth/History/Narrative/Subject/Man/e|e is constituted by an active negation of the Mothers and their many/various/complex/undecidable/multivalent/mater-ial/voi(d)ce.

The Subject of History may be dead, but all of theM-(subaltern)-others—the women, the blacks, the queer, and the poor—in whom power has never resided, still don't have their share of discursive space. Furthermore, they still play a very small part in deciding what even counts as a worthwhile subject of debate. The-M-others of today—the women, the blacks, the queer and the poor—may act 'in the world' more than ever before, but they do so in a man's world, a white, heterosexual, rich man's world.

An all-women's anthology is thus less a demonstration that women can do the same avant-garde, experimental, innovative and conceptual work as men, though they may if they wish. It is a display of the many different avant-garde experimental, innovative and conceptual modes that women themselves conceive.

Feminaissance. It is a small movement. A tiny revolt. But it is not performed in manners determined by self-elected culture-gardes who recognize only one way of being-contemporary. It is a means by which one group of the-M-others, women, may be revolting in their own terms.

This book is dedicated to the all of the-M-others everywhere

> to the women
> the blacks
> the queer
> and the poor.

May your tiniest voidse revolt.

Publishers' and Editor's Foreword
Teresa Carmody, Vanessa Place and Christine Wertheim

This book began as a Cal Arts conference, *Feminaissance: a colloquium on women, writing, experiments, and feminism*, held in 2007 at The Museum of Contemporary Art (MOCA), Los Angeles, with a related workshop and consciousness-raising event at Los Angeles Contemporary Exhibitions (LACE). Many issues were presented and discussed at these events: questions about whether there can be specifically "feminine" forms of text or a specifically *féminine écriture*; notions of selfhood and whether women writers are creating new modes of subjectivity; questions about the social imaginary and its relationship to models of psycho-social organization; notions of gender and feminism, and whether these still hold relevance today; the economic position of women as writers in the academy and marketplace; the history of modern women's writing: mothers, real, symbolic and imaginary; and questions of aesthetics and representation in relation to women's work.

However, the subsequent publication, in the *Chicago Review* 53:2/3 (Autumn 2007) of the paper "Numbers Trouble" presented at the conference by Juliana Spahr and Stephanie Young, lead, in the literary press, to a heated and often acrimonious debate that narrowed the discussion to a single-minded focus on the notion of essentialism and the question of whether a claim to being feminist, or even simply feminine, is compatible with the claim to being avant-garde, innovative, experimental, conceptual, etc.

"Numbers Trouble" is a response to Jennifer Ashton's "Our Bodies, Our Poems," published in *American Literary History*, 19:1 (2007), which is itself partly constructed as a critique of an earlier Spahr and Young piece entitled "foulipo," the text of a performance given at another Cal Arts writing conference, *noulipo*, the anthology of which is published by Les Figues Press (2007). In "Our Bodies, Our Poems" Ashton argues two theses: first, that gender parity has been reached in publishing today, second, that the initial commitment to equality between men and women has been transformed into a commitment to a notion of difference whose bodily focus betrays a logic that is not only "utterly and literally essentialized" (ALH, 228), but also "positively regressive" (AHL, 213). Whilst starting with a brief meditation on the meaning of the term "essentialist," Sphar and Young's response focused steadily on Ashton's first thesis, performing a numerical analysis that shows the lie to her claim. In fact, as their numbers show, less than 40% of published authors are women (at least in the realm of writing that defines itself as avant-garde, experimental, innovative, conceptual, etc.) But despite this admirable research, the debate surrounding the article insisted on discussing Ashton's second thesis, a point barely touched on by Spahr and Young, the question of whether an essentialist position, in this case, the claim to being a specifically feminine or feminist writer, is compatible with being "innovative." (For details of this debate, see "GENDER," at http://www.saidwhatwesaid.com, collected by Erika Staiti.)

Though many interesting points were raised in this debate, very little attention was paid to the notion of essentialism itself, and what it might mean in a contemporary context. Many, if not most, of the writers on both sides simply assumed the concept as self-evident. This failing cannot be held against Spahr and Young, who explicitly acknowledged, in their introduction, the complexity of the question, hence their decision to examine the numbers first. Nor can it be held against Ashton, whose original piece uses the term in a precise way to critique a very specific phenomenon: her perception that what has been defined as "innovative" in post-'80s women's poetry requires the femininity of a poem to be understood as a function of its form, and in which form is seen as a literal translation of the writer's bodily production of the text.

Given the attention this paper and its numbers have received, we felt that the book version of *Feminaissance* should focus on the many other fascinating issues raised at the conference, and on the plurality of voices at play in debates about feminism and writing. At the same time, we wanted to literalize how a discussion of female representation (a discussion which unfortunately continues to be relevant) can mask other discussions about women and writing. On the suggestion of Vanessa Place, we have thus divided the book's pages into three sections. At the top, in bold, is a shortened version of "Numbers Trouble." (Those desiring the text in full may consult the *Chicago Review*.) Below this run two parallel sections across which are distributed the papers and readings given by the other participants of the conference. The whole is punctured by fragments from Lidia Yuknavitch's paper, "psalm," which was structured as a sequence of aphoristic propositions and questions. By this formal means we hope to both preserve the power of Spahr and Young's research, and to highlight the many other important questions raised by contemporary women in relation to notions of feminism and the feminine. This allows for multiple reading strands on each page. It also uses the space of the page as a visual arena for a public conversation: beneath that which is said lies multiple layers of the unsaid. In keeping with this format of multi-vocality we have also partitioned the critical texts into a series of sections marked by •s. This allows for two readings—one continuous, discursive and narrative, the other a more poetic mediation. Thus while each author's paper may be read for its full argument, the sequential blocks offer points for a different kind of reflection.

Essentialism: To Be or Not to Be
Christine Wertheim

An index is a sign whose relation to its referent is existential, as opposed to symbolic or conventional. One indexical relation is causality. An effect is the index of its cause, as say smoke is to fire. Medical symptoms are indices of viruses, or the other conditions producing them. Many clues in detective novels are causal indices. Jennifer Ashton's critique of the repressed relation she detects between poetic form and anatomical morphology, in contemporary women's work that identifies itself as "innovative," is a critique of a causal or indexical mode of thinking. This is what she labels "essentialist," her term indicating a logic that, in spite if its authors' claims to the contrary, defines feminine innovation as a purely bodily affect. Ashton's use of the term is a specification of its more general use: in which identification with a (sub)-section of humanity is linked to an ahistorical, innate idea of some aspect of being. Such links can be made between any (sub)-group and any aspect. I focus here on the more general term, rather than Ashton's narrower one, as it is not possible to engage her argument without first examining the general concept.

Whilst Ashton *argued* her case, that in spite of its authors' conscious ideological positions, innovative women's poetry has unconsciously assumed an innate link between poetic form and the female body, much of the post-Numbers Trouble debate simply took this idea for granted, and then denounced self-identified feminist work on this basis. The reason, I suggest, lies less with an interest in gender, than with a more pressing concern for policing the boundaries of art, for some today believe that we inhabit a post-human age where innovative art is incompatible with identity claims. Thus, any art that claims to speak for or from a specific group is, by definition, retrograde. This argument is profoundly problematic.

At the heart of this view lies the belief that identity is a fiction, a nostalgic throwback to a more romantic age where people and texts were formed round cores of identification with (supposedly) innate features. Though these core identities may once have really inhered, post-humanists argue they can no longer be claimed in the twenty-first century; the up-to-date subject is a man without qualities or identifications of any kind. Of course many people, including artists, still claim specified qualities and allegiances, but these are stuck in the past, and cannot, by definition, be avant-garde. The problem with this notion is that it skirts too quickly round the question of "otherness."

The whole point of the contemporary or post-modern critique of identity was not to dismiss the idea altogether, but to show how all identities are formed in relation to some *other*, or *other-s*. If an identity can never be unified, whole, or self-sufficient this does not make it a fiction. It is simply *relational*. The problem, at least in western society, has been that, not only is the self/I defined as the negation of some Other, but that both self/I and Other are associated with particular kinds of bodies, bodies with particular, and specified attributes. The real problem is how those who have been othered can make sense of their selves? What kind of identities do they have, the many ones who have for so long been cast in the (pro)-position of being the unidentified? By rendering the notion of identity invalid, post-humanists attempt to render every body equal. But every body is not equal. Some bodies, many bodies have never been accorded a recognized identity in western society, and hence are not in a position to lose it, or get over it. Ironically, it is just as some of these others were gaining a sense of their voice that post-humanism arises, once again claiming the vangard status for a privileged elite, and casting those just beginning to speak of/for themselves, the others, as nostalgics destined to fall behind the most advanced units of culture, or at best to repeat an edge that has always already moved elsewhere. But there are other ways to view this matter. Before we completely write off identity, and identification, we should ask what the term "essential" might meaningfully signify in a contemporary or post-post-modern context.

The idea that essentialism is bad is linked to the idea that, if there is no stable essence to identity, the claim to an essential "otherness," defined by identification with a specific set of attributes, is a nostalgic return to, or a longing for, a past ideal. A number of points may be made in relation to *this* ideal:

1. The structural-(ist) theory upon which unstable inessential identity rests disconnects it from both a body and from history. The non- or even anti-essentialized notion of a universal (non)-subject with no specifiable qualities or identifications is the subject of a (pure) disembodied a-historical structure composed of differences in which no-one actually differs at all. This subject is not only unstable and inessential, it is a theoretical fiction.

2. Western history has, as a matter of fact, for decades, centuries, millennia, eons, relegated large swathes of people to the status of being-othered. Thus, even if the position of essential otherness is as constructed as the position of the self-possessed I, the *lived experience* of being treated as, looked upon, called to by the name of the I or the slur of the other transforms this experience in ways that are not pure fictions. As Susan McCabe quotes Marianne Moore, "experience attests/ that men have power/ and sometimes

one is made to feel it." To throw structure back at the structuralists, if meaning is only obtained through the composition of signs, then those signs weigh heavily upon both flesh and the mind. To deny the effect of these bearings is to deny the meaning of meaning, to deny the force of the *power* in the structure. For while structures may be composed of arbitrary differences disconnected from referents, the elements thereby differentiated are not arbitrarily or equally valorized.

3. However much signifiers lack essence, however much most meanings may be said to be unhinged from a referent, some meanings simply are not so unhinged. For instance, however much the traits of a gender may be viewed as cultural constructs, not essential qualities of biology, the fact that some bodies don't bleed unless they're in pain, while others shed blood for the sake of the species, means(!) that the subjects of these bodies live the signifiers of gender differently. The cultural attribution of instability to a body that smells and swells and leaks and gushes out blood, and which may host other smaller bodies, dead and alive, is lived by its "subject," however "structurally neutral," quite differently from the subject of a body that does not do these things. In other words, while gender may be socially constructed, the body is sexed with respect to reproduction, and in every culture, these symptoms attract significations that are laid across, and affect the way embodied subjects live the purely social determinants of gender.

4. Persons, both individual and collective, who have traditionally, that is for a time, and sometimes a long one, been hailed as other, find themselves standing in relation to the contemporary ideal of unstable subjective inessentialism quite differently than those who have traditionally been accorded self-possessed |s. In other words, on this subject, time counts.

These considerations lead to a reassessment of the essentialist question, not just to its solutions, but to the question itself.

The subject of a body that, for whatever reason—skin-color, height, geographical placement, anatomical function in the reproduction of the species—has traditionally been designated some (kind of) other, may find itself split between the yearning to be contemporary and unqualified, and an allegiance with its traditional specified, albeit socially constructed group. And this, not because it is merely "nostalgic." Rather, because the value system that creates in a subject the desire to be anti-essential is itself a force of power; a force that operates through colonizing desire. (I am indebted to Stephania Pandolfo for the particular formulation of the split subject outlined here. Though

Pandolfo develops her ideas in order to make sense of post-colonial mental patients, I believe her analysis may be equally applied to the condition of many contemporary "others" including women.)

Such a subject is doubly split and doubly caught. First, in the time of an unpresent state between a fictional past and an anterior future that it will never achieve; second, between its desire for autonomy and its longing for continued adherence to its identification with a collective.

This split subject, temporally caught between a past that never really(!) was, and a present it can never attain, for this past will always have moved on before the double-one catches up, a subject at once both contemporary and nostalgic is a better model of the post-post-modern subject-ideal, than that fictional subject who, never having experienced a split, is certain of its own instability. Indeed, this is the post-post-modern dilemma: any-| who is so clearly certain of anything, including their own lack of qualities, is clearly not unstable enough.

Ergo: a certain degree of ambiguous attachment to an ideal of group identification, that is to a form of (socio-historic) essentialism, is itself one mark of the incertitude necessary to a properly unstable and genuinely contemporary subjective inessentialism.   This includes the in-essentialism of gender identification.

It is with an awareness of *this* more ambiguous, more refined notion of gender and the question of essentialism that *Feminaissance* approaches the question of femininity and its relation to writing, for the subject of this anthology is one who, while she may or may not desire freedom from the bondage of herstory, knows simultaneously that that story is still being told, and that it is not the same as his-story. The pieces in this anthology remind us of the full range of issues vital to women writers today, and the full range of methods they use to explore them. These include: collectivity (Bellamy, Bergvall), *feminine écriture* (Cheng, Kraus); politics and writing (Bergvall, Yuknavitch, Bellamy); text and voice (Morris); the body as a site of contestation, insurgence and pleasure (Cheng, Kapil, Bellamy); race and writing (Morris, Coleman); relations between subjects and objects (Place); gender as performance (Myles, Kraus, Spahr); women writers (McCabe, Bergvall, Nelson, Morris); the economics of gender (Coleman); Hélène Cixous (Cheng, Bergvall, Kapil); writing pedagogy (Morris); monstrosity (Kapil, Cheng); madness (Kraus); aesthetics (Place, Bergvall). The book is thus neither an exhaustive survey, nor a summary of any field. It is a snapshot, a small slice through the vast confection that is women's writing today. We hope it continues the debate by inspiring others to make their own contributions.

FEMINAISSANCE

Where are the Whitmans? The Steins?
– Lidia Yuknavitch

In "Our Bodies, Our Poems," Jennifer Ashton argues that while corrective anthologies that concentrate solely on writing by women made a certain sense in

The Feminist Writers' Guild
Dodie Bellamy

"I don't know whether we were feminists. We did establish political positions in our class by picking best friends." —Kathy Acker, *My Mother Demonology*

In her book *Intimate Revolt*, Julia Kristeva argues that the "new world order," which Guy Debord characterizes as "the society of the spectacle," is not conducive to revolt. "Against whom can we revolt," she asks, "if power is vacant and values corrupt?" In order to nurture a healthy questioning of the status quo, she proposes "tiny revolts." "[W]e have reached the point of no return, from which we will have to re-turn to the little things, tiny revolts, in order to preserve the life of the mind and of the species." Addressing the feminist movement, Kristeva suggests that "after all the more or less reasonable and promising projects and slogans," feminism's great contribution has been a "revalorizing of the sensory experience." Of course we could argue with this, we could say "how patronizing," we could shake our fingers at Kristeva's lengthy analyses of Barthes, Sartre, Aragon, and ask, why doesn't she add at least one woman to the mix. We could mutter about her stilted, abstract

---

"Say Did You See that Wind from the East": a feminist is
Susan McCabe

In *What is Remembered*, Alice B. Toklas recorded her last hours with Stein:

> By this time Gertrude Stein was in a sad state of indecision and worry. I sat next to her and she said to me early in the afternoon, "What is the answer?" I was silent. "In that case," she said, "what is the question?"[1]

I begin with Stein because she is the precursor to many poststructuralist conceptions of art, identity, epistemology, not to mention the mother of experimental poetry; I should also say that feminism is the disvalued mother of much of postmodern theory, from queer to post-colonial. Stein generated a body of work devoted to, among other things, the "performance of gender identity" and to exposing Realism's false pretence to true representation. As is well-known, she boasted that she had made the rose new for the first time since Shakespeare through her motto: "A rose is a rose is a rose," a phrasing that

the 1970s, "by the mid-80's efforts to 'redress the imbalance' had apparently succeeded. She thus argues that the continued anthologizing of "innovative"

style—like how sensual is that? But in her own way, Kristeva approves of feminism here. She lauds the sensory intimacy that arises out of "the universe of women" for it offers "an alternative to the robotizing and spectacular society that is damaging the culture of revolt."

•

Reading the first couple of chapters of *Intimate Revolt* got me rethinking the Feminist Writers' Guild, the short-lived U.S.-based political action group. I'm not sure exactly when the Guild was founded, but its national newsletter was published from 1978 through 1987. Whenever I've written about my late '70s involvement with the Bay Area chapter, I've presented the group as rather dopey. Here's an example from my essay, "Low Culture":

> When we published an anthology of members' work, we held our editorial meetings naked in a hot tub in Berkeley, and we collated the printed pages, naked on a deck in Marin. I got sunburned on parts of my body that had never before seen the light of day. Compared to these lusty gals, I was a bit of a

---

embellished the ceiling of the Stein/Toklas chamber. In her hermeneutic circle, Stein pared the rose down to its linguistic roseness—eluding definitional closure. Yet *roses* do not *merely* perform roseness anymore than women merely perform gender—it is truly impossible to remove the dancer from the dance; we may not pretend to know the rose in essence, yet some form of phenomenological experience persists. A feminist is a feminist is a feminist; a lesbian is a lesbian is a lesbian. And yet. This is not to argue for a totalizing figure; yet I suggest we may need these identifications insofar as they express something others might prefer to erase. Postmodern patriarchy, that baggy creature of unknown dimensions, would have us live in a shooting gallery with fake targets; it would remain unnamed and unlocated, iterating: *there is no self; no source; no origin for literal and psychic gender oppression; no experience.* Marianne Moore's "Marriage," a long collage poem (presumably without center or fixed self) often occurs to me as an excellent rejoinder, especially her lines, "experience attests / that men have power / and sometimes one is made to feel it."[2]

•

writing by women is essentialism. In addition to the women's poetry anthologies of the 1990s and beyond—Maggie O'Sullivan's *Out of Everywhere: Linguistically*

shrinking violet. My first poetry reading was arranged by Gloria Anzaldúa. It was with the owner of the Marin sundeck, a woman who went by the name of Abigail Tigresslily. Abigail began with a rather ecstatic piece about her big dog going down on her—and then when she got to human-to-human sex, she used the word "slurp." I was horrified, more by slurp than the dog.

Publishing collective, uptight me naked with a bunch of women, bestiality, my inauguration into the public sphere—reading this now through the breathless lens of French theoretical nostalgia, I'm struck by the radical potential of these "lusty gals," how in the culture of the Guild the business of writing, marketing, group process itself is shot through with sensuality and the body. I wonder if what I've been seeing as dopiness isn't in fact the epitome of Kristeva's tiny revolts.

•

In 1979, six of us formed a publishing collective. We took a 10-week course in offset printing, and for our class project printed an anthology of our work entitled *Danaid*, whose name comes from the Latin for Monarch butterflies. In Greek

---

In a 2006 forum in a *PMLA* [journal] devoted, oddly, refreshingly, to feminism, Toril Moi's essay, "'I am Not a Feminist, But...': How Feminism Became the F-Word," attributes some of the fear in taking on feminism's mantle to the widespread successful campaign of conservative extremists in the 1990s media, including Rush Limbaugh's "popularizing the term 'feminazis.'"[3] Moi also asserts: "[t]he fundamental assumptions of feminist theory in its various current guises . . . are still informed by some version of post-structuralism. No wonder, then, that so much feminist work today produces only tediously predictable lines of argument. // This is not a problem for feminist theory alone. The feeling of exhaustion. Of domination by a theoretical *doxa* that no longer has anything new to say, is just as prevalent in non feminist theory." (1736-7)

•

Little paragraph: Theory *can* exhaust the life out of the very revolution in gender thinking it helped foster; similarly does theory threaten to impoverish art, if it loses itself in the abstraction of a continual denial *of all grounds* of self, identification, materiality, embodiment.

***Innovative Poetry by Women in North America and the U.K.*, Mary Margaret Sloan's *Moving Borders: Three Decades of Innovative Writing by Women*, and**

myth the Danaids are the daughters of the Earth and the moon goddess. We were struck with the notion that "although there were only three, their might was such that mythology called them fifty." The cover sports a wrap-around photo, printed in purple ink, of a zillion Monarch butterflies. In publishing the anthology, we too were mighty, shedding our cocoons. Even though we were publishing ourselves, in forming our collective, "we would be able to promote the writing of *all* women: lesbian and straight, women of all colors, ages, backgrounds." I'm quoting from the mission statement we published as the introduction to *Danaid*.

Before the collective settled down to just the six of us, when it was still an amorphous group of maybe-I'm-interesteds, each meeting would devolve into long, heated arguments over whether or not quality of the writing should be a concern in editing a feminist publication. Feminism was about promoting and encouraging all women. Editing for quality would reinscribe patriarchal hierarchies. And who dare define what's quality and what isn't, anyway? Someone would invariably say something like, "Come on, get realistic, we don't want a crappy anthology," and then came the racist and classist accusations. Women would spurt tears of frustration, anger, hurt. These arguments bored me

---

To say that "feminism" is no longer operable is to desert the ship before it has set sail. I might go so far as to say we exist in a pre-feminist Age.

•

Susan Stanford Friedman's "Diary: the Future of Feminism," (also in the *PMLA* issue of 2006), presents an "experiment in juxtaposition and collage": a series of letters Friedman received from feminist students and scholars in Iraq who are starved for a larger discussion about modernist texts and ideas. These letters help the H.D. scholar (and us) resituate modernism, shifting the focus to the now "current burning of Baghdad, the city of Scheherazade, the great metropole of the vast cultural, scientific, and commercial Islamic empire that reached from China to Spain long before the rise of Western forms of modernity." (1706) *A Thousand and One Nights*, with its multiple composite narratives of suspense, prefigures the modernist feminist as well as the Iraqi blogger, Riverbend, whose *Baghdad Burning: Girl Blog from Iraq* was published by the Feminist Press in 2005, a text Friedman uncovers and teaches. "Feminist analysis," Friedman nicely remarks, "is no longer the central conceptual focus but rather a stance that infuses the

Claudia Rankine and Juliana Spahr's *American Women Poets of the 21st Century*—she also charges Kathleen Fraser, Rachel Blau DuPlessis, and Lyn

at the time, as I sat on the floor drunk and stoned, but now I look back on them with awe, the overtness, the trying to work through differences, the belief that classism was bad.

●

At the back of *Danaid* there is a group photo of the six of us sitting in front of a printing press. I'm on the far right, my hair falls to my shoulders and I'm wearing my Tibetan wrap-around, maroon-colored, or perhaps cranberry in today's parlance. My eyes are round and vacant, I'm staring but don't seem to be seeing anything, so caught up in my own interiority I'm impenetrable. Such withdrawal is my knee-jerk response to group situations. One therapist told me I had "reverse charisma." Abigail sits beside me, her arm resting on my thigh, laughing, looking at me with delight, suggesting that just before this photo was taken something amusing transpired between us, that I was present for a moment, then the lens clicks and I'm gone.

At 28 I hadn't been civilized yet—I was a blur of raw emotions, ranging from the ecstasy of encountering a particularly beautiful day to panic attacks

---

whole." (1707) In other words, feminism need not be a totalizing movement. Yet urgently, Scheherazade must tell her stories, again and again, to keep alive, a trans-global feminist muse.

●

Stein, a kind of Scheherazade writing through the night and into the dawn, began again and again. She felt alarm at names too—like some of my students—afraid of spelling out the "F," "L" and "P" words. One of Stein's most overtly feminist and lesbian works—*Lifting Belly*—is also one of her most anti-nationalist poems. After the war broke out in 1914, Gertrude and Alice spent the spring and summer of 1915 in Majorca, a Mediterranean setting replete with the sensuous—fig trees, the ocean, fish, almonds, sun, but also in the distance, a German ship. Posthumously published, *Lifting Belly* rewrites the National Anthem through her transmutable, fragmentary lines:

>   *Say did you see that wind from the east.*
>   *We used to play star spangled banner.*
>   *Say that you see that you are praised.*
>   *What can you say.*

Hejinian with this same essentialism. // Our [first] reaction to this article was a combination of annoyance and confusion, and also moments of agreement. We

that left me doubled over. "It's like there's this horse inside my solar plexus," I said to Cindy over the phone, "bucking to get out." "Dodie," she said, "let me come over and get you." We weren't lovers, but when I was frightened or lonely, Cindy would take me into her bed and hold me. I've parodied Cindy more than once in my writing. She appears as a straight woman with a penchant for lesbian spectacle, toying with my hair and coming on to me in public. She wore her Southerness, too, like a gaudy accessory. A product of private schools and psychotherapy, even though she was raised in New Orleans, she never tasted gumbo until some guy served it to her in San Francisco, then she was all over filé powder. "Dodie, let me come and get you." The generosity of her body pressing calmness into mine, heartbeat, breath, arms, in out, in out. In our group photo, Cindy's gaze is locked on the camera, as if to say, "All mine."

•

Memory: Finally breaking up with my on again off again long term lover over the phone while spending the night at Abigail's. Crying and shivering—it gets cold at night in Marin—on the futon in the guest room, which was lined with

---

> *Can you sing.*
> *Can you.*
> *Can you can you.*
> *Can you buy a Ford.*
> *Can you say winking.*
> *When this you see remember me.*
> *When this you see remember me.*
> *We will remember.*
> *When this you see you will kiss me.*[4]

Stein's dialogue suspends the singular ego's and nation's claim to solidity; it is exchangeable, vehicular, yet historical. Stein knew that the effort to name things, once and for all, is an absurdist exercise. Still from *Lifting Belly*:

> *What is a man.*
> *What is a woman.*
> *What is a bird.*

•

began by talking about representational practices. Then we talked about economics, that is, the publication and lauding of works with prizes rather than

books and thus called "The Virginia Woolf Memorial Library." When Abigail and her lover get up the next morning, I'm still awake, red-eyed and sniveling. "Why didn't you wake us," she says in exasperation. I didn't trust her. She had all this money, she called herself a Dianic priestess, she used to write speeches for Nixon, when her lover became involved with Susan Griffin, the way she would say with relish, "Susan Griffin stole my girlfriend." Susan Griffin—I remember her standing near a staircase with her blonde bangs, the chandelier in the foyer beams down on her and she glows like a goddess. This was the first time I'd been in the same room with someone famous who I hadn't paid to see. Beneath Abigail's affectations, I sensed a deep and abiding craziness, a white hot radical core. She and the other Guild members led me into a feminist dreamscape. In those wood-laden living rooms in Berkeley and Marin, behind the bay windows in Gloria Anzaldúa's San Francisco commune, Bloomsbury reawakened. We were feminists, we were larger than life, our actions, our words mattered. We would go down in history.

•

I am told that some of the artists in the WACK exhibit didn't want to identify themselves as primarily feminists. Denial erupts also... *I am not a feminist...* in almost every trans-gender experiment or so-called feminist work: one might think of Djuna Barnes, in spite of her famous lesbian classic *Nightwood*, disavowing: *I am not a lesbian, I only loved Thelma*. Passing strange, even without looking here at the possible contradictions between feminism and calling oneself a lesbian, a breed my significant other thinks is becoming obsolete, like squires in the 19th century. Think of another later form of hiding, written in the '70s: *If only I had been a woman* says Elizabeth Bishop's tongue-in-cheek persona, Crusoe. Why do artists renounce identification with a name, a movement? *What is my other name*, incanted Stein. *I too dislike it*, Moore writes of poetry, and what she disliked were the expectations that came with poetry; she wanted to carve out a new place for female wit and the poetic imagination.

•

A man a woman a bird.
What is it about names that makes us want to throw them off?

the ways gender gets represented in writing. Every time we started talking about who gets published, who wins prizes, and who gets academic jobs, we basically

How did it all end? I got involved with some students from the San Francisco Art Institute, I started taking workshops with more experimental writers. I was voracious for experience and sophistication—the artists and avant gardists seemed hipper, more exciting, and they did encourage me to write—but never again would I receive such uncomplicated acceptance from a community; never again would my vacant stares, weirdness, social dysfunction be held with such tenderness; never again would I experience an arts community whose mandate was inclusivity.

•

Memory: Thanksgiving at Abigail's, picking baby lettuce from her garden, filling her sink and swishing the dirt from the tiny leaves, smoking really good grass, so good the food felt foreign, sitting at her long rough-hewn dinner table, staring down at thick, foreign cream soup. Memory: Walking with Abigail and her big dog, whose name was Artemis, along a hilly dirt road in Tiburon. It's a hot day, not quite twilight, lush vegetation folds in on us in every direction, wild life scampers, Abigail whips off her T-shirt and takes in the gorgeousness bare-

---

Mary Daly's *Gyn/Ecology*, radical feminist best seller yet almost submerged in the chasm between the second-wave and now, clarifies: "patriarchy is the ruling religion of the planet."[5] Many of my students are hesitant to utter the "p-word" because such utterances are thought to be naïve. But what are they dodging?

•

Recently, I was at a dinner party; everyone was laughing and arguing. One asked: could we imagine Frank O'Hara writing certain of his poems without his being gay? Another claimed his poems reflected the *universal imagination*. What about Ginsberg, I tossed out, trying to alleviate the rising tension. By the time the main course was over, several of the dinner guests had agreed, sipping their coffees that all poets were "gay." O'Hara let people like gayness. It sounds so clever in his work. Lesbians have had a much harder time being liked. This is not to say, of course, that gay men have not suffered from a patriarchal and homophobic culture; it is just to say that lesbians (or rather lesbian poets) do not usually wear their gayness with an alluring sang-froid or magnetic marginality. We are not all gay in the same way.

•

ended up lost in a tailspin of contradictions. // And then we began to wonder, did the numbers support Ashton's claims or not? // One reason that this

breasted. I feel both irritated with her staginess and envious. There's no fucking way I could do this, but Abigail creates within me this little kink, I want to display my body with her ease, want to ram it down my readers' throats, rather than always hunching over, hiding, hiding.

•

Need the success of a political group be measured by its impact on a larger social order? What about the ways it transforms the lives and psyches of its members—these tiny revolts—are they not profound? As Macy Gray sings in her anthem "Sexual Revolution," "Time to be free amongst yourselves" for your "freak" is "a beautiful thang." I pick up *Danaid* and read my author bio. My clichéd rhetoric embarrasses me. I proclaim myself, for example, "the daughter of a carpenter and strong woman." Then I get to, "She has been writing poetry since the age of 14. While writing has always been an important part of her life, it has often been pushed in the background in favor of more 'practical' considerations, such as the monotony of graduate school or full-time labor. In the past year, Dodie has made the decision to make writing her top priority."

The feminism I imagine keeps its bodies and identities, its experiments. Rather simplistically, we need the categories of gender until conditions that continue to divide along gender lines disappear—and further, women have to make space for their perspectives, or else they will find themselves watching yet one more buddy movie.

A feminist is a fluxist is a bird. To be like. We know there are women torturers. So it goes. It's not about substitution. Can't stand in the same river twice.

•

Penultimate paragraph. Mr. Hemingway was repulsed when he heard the word "pussy" filtering down from Stein's upstairs bedroom. Stein's mulatta character Melanctha was so blue she didn't know what to do and "wandered widely" making trouble and gained her "wisdom" of polymorphous and lesbian sexuality, always a given of Stein's art. Stein couldn't have written what she had without the collaborative intimacy and anti-patriarchal stance she shared with Toklas.

•

question interests us so much is that we feel her dismissal of female community formations parallels a larger cultural dismissal of feminism that shows up in

After toying with writing for 14 years, I was finally wrenching it from the black hole of hobby. What I learned in that hot tub, sun deck, those Arts and Crafts houses, was possibility, commitment. I was young, fucked up, frightened, working class, I was faking it as a graphic artist, a job I had neither training nor aptitude for, I was a misplaced Midwesterner, maybe I was lesbian or maybe I wasn't, but first and foremost I was a writer and come hell or high water the world would listen to me. When we published an anthology of members' work, we destroyed the capitalist system from within. Naked, gloriously wet, we blazed like jewels, our tiny spasms of revolt burned the sun, boggled the mind. To you it may have looked like a hot tub but to those blessed with feminist vision it was a coracle floating down the river Canaan, we were violets, we were tigers, we wrote and fucked like dogs, we roasted turkeys stoned out of our minds, we read poetry, brought roses, curled in bed together like shrimp, double breasted, double fisted, we slurped up patriarchy in our lily-throated cunts. Moonfaced, smeared with purple butterfly ink, we answered the phone for one another, we were open to all.

There are feminists and there are feminists. The now reclaimed feminist, Mina Loy, exulted in the blood and guts of the surgical room when she was a nurse during WW-I. She said that under analgesic the men called her a lot worse than Madonna. Her 1914 feminist manifesto called for "unconditional surgical destruction of virginity through-out the female population at puberty" to abolish the "fictitious value" of purity (through the literal hymen), and thereby "the division of women into two classes the mistress, & the mother."[6] She demanded: "Leave off looking to men to find out what you are not—seek within yourselves to find out what you are." (154) An attractive point among the nettles. There is, however, a problem lurking in over-literalizing psychical and imaginative experience. Scheherazade lives among the ruins and the flames. She is a muse to many as she disappears and comes to life in the shadow of her own narrative. The "apparitional lesbian" might indeed have something going for her—if she can exist in a flux of her own making, with her self-identifications flashing like scimitars. *And yet* one is a feminist and one is not. Again and again, I remind myself that pleasure is a part of taking on and taking off a name. Stein will have hers as affinity, question and caress:

peculiar and intense ways in contemporary writing communities, often in the name of progressive politics. Instead of Ashton, we could point to the well

Works Cited:

Bellamy, Dodie. "Low Culture." *Narrativity*, Issue 3. 2003. http://www.sfsu.edu/~poetry/narrativity/issue_three/bellamy.html

Danaid: An Anthology of Six Women Writers. Berkeley: The Mariposa Press, 1979.

Kristeva, Julia. *Intimate Revolt.* New York: Columbia University Press, 2002.

Do you like ink.
Better than butter.
Better than anything.
Any letter is an alphabet.
When this you see you will kiss me.
Believe it is for pleasure that I do it.

Works Cited:

1. Alice B. Toklas. *What is Remembered.* San Francisco: North Point Press, 1985.
2. Marianne Moore. "Marriage." *The Poems of Marianne Moore*, ed. Grace Schulman. New York: Viking Press, 2003. 160.
3. Toril Moi. "'I am Not a Feminist, But…': How Feminism Became the F-Word." *PMLA* 121-5, 2006.1736.
4. Gertrude Stein. *Lifting Belly.* Tallahassee: Naiad Press, 1989. The lines I quote from the text are taken from throughout—and do not follow consecutively in Stein's text.
5. Mary Daly. *Gyn/Ecology: The Metaethics of Radical Feminism.* Boston: Beacon Press, 1990. 124.
6. Mina Loy. *The Last Lunar Baedeker.* New York: Farrar Straus Giroux, 1996. 154-5.

meaning but dismissive lefty claim of Ron Silliman's 1998 "Poetry and the Politics of the Subject" that manages to write women out of any history of

from *Incubation: a space for monsters*
Bhanu Kapil

TEXT TO COMPLETE A TEXT

Sex is always monstrous. Blood appears in the air next to the body but nobody asks a question about the body. "Please touch me there. More. Oh god." For a hitchhiker, the problem of the boudoir is transferred to a makeshift, itchy, unsafe space on the verge of a New Mexico highway. It is often the sex of another era, in which the socks and dress shirt/blouse are not necessarily removed.

I hitchhiked in the beginning because it seemed glamorous to me, ultra-American, like a Christian with an entrenched migraine who resorts to brand-name anti-inflammatories when prayer does not do the trick. At first, my encounters on the thoroughfares of your country were quotidian; after all, it is not really hitch-hiking to buy a greyhound ticket three weeks in advance then have a going-away party in a dorm with a banner and balloons. Again, this is an

---

tapestry
Eileen Myles

Rose was number one. Fairly light hair on a warm young mound. Later I knew this poet from Boston, and he lived in a loft in Little Italy with a girl who made art. Their life seemed perfect. And she was number two—I got her. She was like a welder or something, though she was small. Not tiny, but slight. Not really skinny, but normal looking, beautiful. She was a little beaky, but with beautiful breasts. We started palling around. She admired my straight leg jeans and Chinese shoes, immediately she got the same. When I think of our friendship we are walking in the rain, getting the toes of our shoes wet in puddles. After they broke up she quietly called and wanted to hang out. I couldn't believe that I was soon taking her pants down on my bed. She liked to drink booze. I remember her smiling face looking down into a glass with about an inch of whiskey. She wore glasses. She took them off and she was hot. Clits were all different. Hers was larger. All rubbery, more like porn. I had seen a pussy like hers before but not so close. It was like a lip going vertical. I mean, if you had your head right

formal innovation when he argues that the writing of "women, people of color, sexual minorities, the entire spectrum of the 'marginal' [...] should often appear

example of departure in another time. As a foreign student on a scholarship, it was an ordinary matter to file for an extension for the completion of a thesis on Salman Rushdie's early works. Nevertheless: "How can we keep tabs on these JI visa holders, who come over here and…the university, as an institution, really needs to be more accountable. We need a database and we need a system of checks and balances to make sure any change of address is verified by at least two pieces of information. They need to do their course work and then they need to go home."

I didn't want to go home. This is a boring sentence. Perhaps for you Oregon is a calming word, evoking images of blackberry pie, ocean vistas and the capture of suspected felons. I had never heard the word Oregon before. Like the distance of Scotland from London, it seemed impossibly far. A beautiful hazard: to go and keep going. How can I put this? In England, nobody ever, ever, ever did this. I, who once drove straight to Glasgow with a thermos of instant coffee mixed with milk and sugar, in a dinged up Datsun Cherry, was considered an anomaly. "Are you demented? Why do you want to drive in a car to bloody Scotland? It's

---

there. It was kind of a lippy trail, actually this is not her clit, it's her labia I'm describing, what I used to describe as a little girl my gum. Outer gum. Hers was a very uncomplicated female and large a red road to a small swollen button. I kept thinking I can't believe she feels this way about me. She came over to do this. I put my two fingers on the spot and rubbed. I have always been an unpredictable masturbator, spending hours for naught. Getting huge, and then having to go out in pain. Then I'll touch myself for a second in a public toilet (New York Public Library, always great) and the walls of the world cave in. So I was just kind of scrubbing away, moving her jelly part, not the button itself the way it hangs, it wiggling sits. She groaned. It was a teeny way she sounded when she looked at art, but this was a deeper older oh. She was a woman. One by one the women I knew who seemed to be girls, or men, or just strangers—when all their muscles tensed then released, and they said oh it was like the deepest voice they had. Like the secret room behind all the other apartments now connected to mine. This oh. I didn't think of it then, but I think of it now, all the guy poet's fake ohs. Next to this one so female and true. Is that what man wants to do. Oh Brazil. O New York. O Poetry! Just let me come like her. She got mad. You can

much more conventional" because they are marginalized and the marginalized need to tell their stories. Or one could refer to how so many of the single gender

seven hours on the M1, man!" Though, outwardly, I was wan and somewhat reticent, I…no, I was. My sexual experience consisted of lying under an elm tree in Hyde Park at the age of seventeen and being told by an undergraduate student of the London School of Economics that my breasts in that position, from that angle, resembled two fried eggs. We were meeting in a park as per the era. I am sure contemporary Punjabi-British teenagers are fearless individuals, undaunted by the prospect of community censure. Back then we met by the iron wrought gate on a park bench, on a path built for seventeenth century promenades. It is always a century. In my century sex was a field of restraint and intensity unsurpassed by anything except drinking coffee in a foreign country like Scotland or Wales and borrowing my father's car forever. "Are you out of your bleeding head? Your dad's going to skin you alive!"

In some senses, this (driving) is the opposite of hitchhiking, in which the interior of the car is always unfamiliar. Then this day was real in a different way, in the way that it sensitized me to risk, a kind of twin to permission. Two black swans: that day and this one, history and fiction, what I went for and what I really

---

stop. I mean I sort of knew, but I wasn't sure. Between women if you're having sex, you've got to be sure. And slowly that's where you live. Who wouldn't give up being in a whole lot of shitty poetry magazines for this. Chris had rough black hair on her crotch. It got rougher when she drank all the time. I began to think of her pussy as an animal. We tended its coat. I was always willing to have sex with her, but I liked it better when she was pretty and clean. One woman was told by a lover that she had a fat cooch. It was true—her outer lips were pillowy and fat. Full. Her inner lips were regulation healthy and her clit—it was a small red little spud. It was however guardian of one of the most avid pussies I've ever known. Not the biggest, but damn the most willing, most sporting. I fucked her once for ten hours straight. She puked and she wanted to continue. I would never be allowed to sleep. I was hallucinating. I used this hand, then that. Fingers individually, in groups and my whole fucking hand, again and again. I used my dick. It was a nice fat boy, rather featureless which at the time seemed correct, a white guy who appeared out of the fly of my overalls, I was being a farmer boy and when she felt it wagging between my legs as I bent over her in front of a fire, her eyes lit up. Thanks to the fire I was able to see this glory. She

anthologies apologize for their existence. Even Mary Margaret Sloan, in a sentence that Ashton echoes, concedes about *Moving Borders*, "perhaps a book

wanted, which I didn't know until I got there by which time it was impossible to consider the long journey home as either practical or sensible, considering the trouble I was already in and the rain, which had started to come down in a series of reddish sheets; the streetlamps were pink.

On Prince Street, in Glasgow, I saw the sign for American style pizza and went down the steps to the basement café. The tables were coated with green plastic. There was hot tea, which the waitress slung down my gullet with a funnel as I focused my eye on a laminated print of a white, blocky rose with a pink dot at its center. "Charles Rennie Mackintosh," said the waitress, so that the last sound in the name—"osh"—rhymed with horse. "Are you from India?" "Would you like some jam with that scone? I bet they don't have scones in India, do they?" "More tea? I heard you have a lot of tea, over there, isn't that right?"

Plan b: The extension of my throat. The euphoria of theft. Other countries with their sayings and beliefs. The original plan, formulated by my father during his morning commute across London: Marrying a British-born Hindu Brahmin

---

told me that she landed in a hospital once because she had urged her boyfriend to fuck her while she was hanging out a 23rd story window of a huge apartment building in Manhattan. Apparently this high intensity fucking caused some kind of lump in the walls of her vagina and she wound up in the hospital where she learned something or other that was sad.

But she was in there for fucking. I mean that's pretty good. There was a small woman who had a lacy looking pussy that she hated. There was like this frottage over her clit. Instead of a hood it had a large mantilla. She wasn't the kind of woman who could laugh at her puss. It made her sick what she considered her irregularity, the wave of skin that dangled between her legs. I would have told her it was pretty if she let me. It was unique. She was not a girl even slightly about letting, allowing suffering anything at all. She had levels of protection like the shaft of an elevator. She was way up there somehow, unknown but looking down like a little girl incredibly mean who could issue commands. After her orgasms, screaming *ugh*. Then I met a woman who described her clit as a monster. There is nearly no woman who regards her pussy as normal. I remember seeing a pussy I recognized on the back outside cover of an art magazine. It was like

such as this marks an occasion when, at the end of a period of historical transition, such a book is no longer necessary. A barrier has been crossed; a

dentist with brown skin, but not too brown, and rosy cheeks. Note on the mantelpiece, tucked behind the marble figurine of Shiva: What is forthcoming under the original plan? Extraction? What kind of sex is possible on the dentist's chair late at night for that girl, your girl, who nervously asks for a blanket? She has her socks on. She's shivering. It is sometimes sex when you touch yourself beneath the proffered blanket clearly not washed between patients, but in this scene the limbs of the dentist's young Asian bride are rigid and smell faintly of wintergreen-scented nail polish or mouthwash. Dad, "please don't swallow." Rinse then spit. Spit then swallow.

I could not go home and so, after a brief visit to the Hill House—Charles Rennie Mackintosh's art deco home on the Firth of Clyde, where he painted geometric rosebuds forever in a kind of frenzy, as it seemed from the décor—I turned left and kept driving. I drove my car into the Atlantic and kept driving, my chest very tight beneath the surface. It was difficult to feel anything or really to see, and so I can only say that I went into a damaging ocean. This is going. Damaged, washed up on the mythical shores of New Jersey a few days later, my car failed to

---

it was supposed to be a big secret whose pussy it was. I mean they didn't say her name underneath though they did give you the name of the photographer which was kind of a hint. But then everyone said oh yeah, you saw the picture of blank's pussy, like everyone was really in on it. But I recognized the pussy. I actually knew her tits better than her pussy, because her tits were that kind that are indented, the tip of the nipple goes in, not out. Which is incredibly common, or else coincidentally I had two such breasts' (or girlfriends) back to back which made me think it must be common. The first one's did look odd to me. I can't imagine what straight women do, going through life only being looked at by men and doctors. At some point you always have to have a frank conversation about the tits or the puss, or the ass. If you live with her you have it day in and day out. Maybe men do this too. The girl I described as extraordinarily hungry—she in fact regarded her puss with the same enthusiastic love as any other part of her, perhaps that was her oddity (to me). Her pussy was no more special than her fingertips or cheek. Sexually she was entirely alive, so neither liked nor disliked her clit, it was *her*. It was the whole rest of the world she had a problem with, so it was great she had this gift, her wonderful successful body. The woman who

roughly equivalent number of women and men are publishing the most significant and demanding innovative work at the moment." // So at this point

start. This is later, when the car stopped and looking up from my hands, white-knuckled on the steering wheel, I realized that I was okay.

Now I am here, in the future of color. I'm sorry I do not have more to say about the period of submergence that preceded my arrival. I am not interested in it. I do not recall it. I… It was only when my car stopped that I realized what I had to do, on my own terms, with my own two legs: Get going. Is that how you say it? Get up and go. The destiny of my body as separate to my childhood: I came here to hitchhike. I came here to complete a thing I began in another place. Removing wet pages from my rucksack, I lay them on the shore, securing them with beautiful shells and pebbles. When they dried, I folded them into squares and put them in my pocket, next to my body. Misshapen, exhilarated, I said get. I said go. Get up now and go. "Are you okay?" "Do you need a ride somewhere?" "Let me look in the trunk. I might have something in there. Here you go. You're shivering! Do you need to go to the hospital? At least let me buy you a cup of coffee."

---

regarded hers as monstrous nonetheless is entirely addicted to hers. I was too. The tiny shelf of skin I slipped my tongue and finger alongside of, it's like the backside of a rubber duck. And so I knew my sweet toy's edges in the dark quietly going to sleep with ducky in mind. The hood of it was slick, so she had a small cap between her legs, a bullet of pleasure and power. Even after she had one of her outrageous sunset orgasms which she details while still basking in its immense succulent corona slowly with an utterly generous and female smile on her face, a satisfied smile and kind, she urges me to put my finger on her secret fingertip and feel the blood pump as the pleasure is ebbing away. She's always ready for a nap and then to go again. She's always just finding it. Every time we fuck she forgets that its ever been that great before. Her eyes are closed and she proclaims that never, never before has she experienced anything to even remotely approach what *that* felt like. Does sex ever feel like this for a man. Does his tree change and spout. Does his system get up, does he go. I once was laying in bed with her and she got me off just by touching and I am still sinking backwards in that picture, a morning in which I lie in bed looking out the window at a passing train.

we did several things. We attempted to construct a history of the experimental/
postmodern/avant-garde/innovative scene and then started to count its men and

> If we are writers, we want to be legitimized,
> even by illegitimate sources.
>
> It bothers me less and less that I cannot achieve legitimacy
> from illegitimate sources.

Two Poems
Tracie Morris

My mammy my mammy my mammy my mammy my mammy my mammy
   my mammy my *Ma*n
My mammy my mammy my mammy my mammy my mammy my mammy
   my mammy my *Ma*n
Is Guarded guarded Guarded guarded Guarded guarded Guarded guarded
   Guarded guarded Guarded guarded Guarded guarded Guarded guarded
      Guarded guarded Guarded guarded gone…
is Dead is dead is dead. is Dead is dead is dead. is Dead is dead is dead. is
   Dead is dead is dead.
is Dead is dead is dead. is Dead is dead is dead. is Dead is dead is dead. is
   Dead is dead instead.

its women. And at the same time, because we figured the numbers would tell only one story and we felt this history could best be written with others, we

Striving to Be a Man:
Gender-Altering Forces in Post-Feminist America
Wanda Coleman

I have managed to survive the 20th century as a literary writer, working in the private sector, most of my adult life, to support my family. One of my favorite quotes has come to be a Jewish saying, "In the world of men, strive to be a man." The first time I heard it, I was struck by the inherent irony in the saying when it was applied to ghetto economics, too often driven by the Single Mom or Grandmother carrying the weight of survival for herself, her children, and/or grandchildren. In my mind's ear, this Jewish quote seemed to pragmatically answer that question so righteously attributed to Sojourner Truth: *Ain't I a woman?* To which I would answer, no—in this situation, sex preference aside, I am striving to be (as capable as) a man.

•

Untitled

What the sister brother mother making in the oven? Subtle shoulder bounce comeuppance? Breakdance from Angolans going, us up under ships rowing? Flowing over undertow, Sammyís taps. Hand jive happenstance to techno trance, folks coveting colored. True black being an encompassing hue, placentas siphoned off magenta, violence, indigo blues with cane cotton tobacco rows to hoe.

So what you sayiní? Sosaís John Henry with a Creatine steam engine? Recidivismís net effect is akin to an Amadou Louima ass kickiní?

Hit it, Reconnoitering Negroes AWOL versus Dominating Nazi Aryans. RNA vs. DNA in the body politic, difference being the leftovers, sugar. What flies is attracted to besides shit. We got some. Circulocutious Infidels affirming the Ferral Biologic importing it.

wrote to a number of people—men and women, although our list was far from inclusive and also somewhat arbitrary—and asked them basically to just tell us

Although part of the African-American subculture, in my desire to be a writer, I fell under the influence of the White world of words and images as it existed in the post World War II era of the 1950s. (Force-fed *I Love Lucy* episodes as a girl, I am probably the only person in America who hates the show and its image of a loveable scatter-brained heroine.) As time went on, and I hungrily consumed western literature, I began to become aware of two major deficits: 1) the absence of Blacklife as I lived it, no representation at all, and 2) the absence of women as I encountered them regardless of race. My initial writing impulses were outgrowths of my desire to fill that double void. Yet, I began by writing in a genderless, voiceless, generic language that reflected the looking-glass universe in which I found myself trapped.

·

Today, as a well-published poet, journalist and writer, I find myself in a peculiarly similar place, despite having developed a distinct voice and style. The issues from which I shape the content of my work certainly seemed important then. On my writing agenda, they became urgencies in the 1960s and '70s. Forty

---

Each territory a precious piece. Kill ëem with kindness. Sweet like a Lauryn declaration of love overlapping the looped Bata backbeat. Like a 12 year oldís pressed curls greased with Dax. Like somebody fifty-seven polishing his T-bird with Turtlewax.

Old romance. Akara to chitlins to chicken wings. Shekere to hambone to two Technics. Field holler Doo Wops make microphone fiends.

a story about poetry and gender. We did not feel that the institutions of poetry were against us, that it was hard for us to get published because we were women,

years later, now, they have become critical if without apparent resolution. It is as though the social movements that helped shape my youth took place in an isolation booth with only a limited volume of the discourse reaching the society beyond. The changes that took place appeared largely cosmetic. Thus, to my dismay, I find that as a 60-year-old woman, I am still regarded as the "nappy headed whore" I was accused of being at age 18. There is less of a place for me in our society in 2007 than there was in 1964.

The O word, in this case, means old as in ancient: Scads of senior citizens, male and female, appear in product endorsements proclaiming a suspect rejuvenation, as with male enhancement products and those battling osteoporosis. However, virtually no women between the ages of 50 and 100 exist in broadcast media. The primary exceptions are to be found in CBS's Katie Couric, Barbara Walters' *The View*, *Martha Stewart Living*, *Oprah*, reruns of the sitcoms *The Golden Girls*, Angela Lansbury as mystery writer and amateur detective Jessica Fletcher on *Murder She Wrote*, and Nancy Marchand as Tony's mother Livia on *The Sopranos*, all on television (where the viewers are predominantly women and African-Americans). America's entertainment industry has openly

---

Continuity
Chris Kraus

"For the truly mad, it's not enough to merely tell stories. They have to act them out."
– Fanny Howe

For *féminine écriture* substitute the words female writing. Not all women writers are female writers, but all female writing is written by women. This is the most concise way I can think of saying it. Perhaps for "female writing" you could substitute the phrase "performative texts"—the text being like a live performance, not a text OF a performance, but the real thing. A text that is both live and lived.

Lived experience implies intensity writes Gilles Deleuze, and intensity is another word for schizophrenia, adds Felix Guattari.

Now there is plenty of schizophrenic writing in the alt.male canon—the ones that come to mind are French: Antonin Artaud, Pierre Guyotat. In the

but we did deal with a lot of gender trouble, a lot of gender dismissal, on a fairly regular basis. [Some of these responses are sited at the end of this paper] //

acknowledged that it caters to the 14-year-old White male psyche (and, to a limited extent, as with *Powerpuff Girls*, its female counterpart).

•

As a working mother, my monetary landscape, regarding salary, is the same. Ironically, the multiculturalism so highly touted in the 1980s has largely meant the status quo. The White males who once acted as the gatekeepers, overseers, and goal tenders have, in many instances, been replaced by women, minorities, or immigrants. In pursuit of the ever-almighty dollar, these groups have also assumed the roles of the oppressors. (I speak unfortunately from experience—formerly as an endowed chair at one of the city's most distinguished campuses, I thought I was being honored until I discovered I was contracted for less than half the salary offered to one of my White male peers, and that the deal was orchestrated by so-called feminists.) Thus, from my perspective, the battleground is fiercely, more intensely, the same. I am, and must be, as ever, concerned with image and self-image in all my demographics:

---

above cases, and all the other cases I can think of, there's always something very histrionic at work, a hefty "I," an overlay of persona, personality. As if the writer has agreed to embark on this CRUSADE of schizophrenia for the benefit of the reader, for the benefit of his art.

•

The schizophrenia of female writing is more pervasive. It doesn't stop. It's sense-surround. And because the schizophrenic state remains a CONSTANT within the condition of being female in this culture (as any woman writing hard enough soon comes to recognize) female writing (re) presents a more generous nimble state of schizophrenia. It's devious, and also more inclusive. If schizophrenia is the state that you're consigned to live in—if you are fated to remain within a universe that's ALL FEELING ALL THE TIME, you have to make it large. Therefore, female writing is extremely intellectual. It is conceptual, but never programmatic. "My brains," writes Ariana Reines, the young genius poet in her debut book, *The Cow*, "could be useful if I didn't force them to feel."

•

What follows is the history that we constructed with the help of those who answered the survey. // Our history starts with Donald Allen's *New American*

> mother
> worker
> black/woman
> writer/human being

•

And I am forced into the continued posture of explainer (or denigrated as whiner). I must continue to gather my energies to fight, as a soldier, in what has been termed "the culture wars." I am embattled on a level deepened by the onset of the digital revolution, agitated by the opening of the regulation and tax floodgates for the rich (thus widening the gap between rich and poor Americans), which fosters the permanent entrenchment of women and children in poverty, and which is sustained by a mass media that has succumbed to the basest elements of human psychology (creating *virtually* a tabloid nation).

•

I marvel at the audacity—the popularity of outfits like Hooters and Victoria's Secret, while aging women comprise the largest segment of American home-

---

Female writing can spazz out in a million directions, but it isn't formalist writing because all these directions lead back to the self. ("The biggest pain in the world is feeling but sharper is the pain of the self," the young Kathy Acker concluded in *Persian Poems*.) Formalist writing abstracts the thinker from thought. Female writing is... more continuous. There is always way too much feeling in female writing, but feeling itself isn't the point. Female writing is compositional. It is intellectual vaudeville. It arrives at the moment of feeling, then leaves. It demonstrates something: itself.

•

In *Rumstick Road*, one of her earliest works, the theater artist Elizabeth LeComte put a two-man domed tent behind the audience. While the protagonist, Spaulding Gray, recalled his mother's mental illness and suicide, with tremendous conviction, center stage, two girls sat in the tent with a flashlight between them and talked. They talked through the entire performance, creating a tremendous pull between the scripted 'drama' and something more ambient. There was something so thrilling about this. Of course I didn't care much about

Poetry, **published in 1960. It is widely accepted as the "seminal" anthology, the one that establishes the current view that U.S. experimental/postmodern/avant-**

less, and glut assisted living and nursing homes. Like observations, with which I have concerned myself over a lifetime, have remained disappointingly constant, hence my writing goals are unchanged:

> to rehumanize the dehumanized
> to use words to bring about change
> to witness, to declare

Yes. Gender still matters. More profoundly than ever.

•

Rather than persist in the resolution of such serious root issues as racism, poverty and health care, America's so-called intelligentsia has capitulated to the inconsequential and public distractions *ad nauseam*. I conclude that the *vox populi* are consumed by them, and, further, believe it is addicted to easy controversies, like the mega-hyped MSNBC controversy in which Don Imus defamed the Rutgers University women's basketball team by satirically calling them "nappy-headed

---

Gray, I couldn't stop watching the girls. The girls were both supporting and undermining the main stage performance. As girls always do.

•

I made a film, *The Golden Bowl or Repression*, which is a kind of female writing. It's 12 minutes long, and amazingly, it took me four years to make it. At that time, there were a lot of girls making this kind of film. There was an idea, there was a feeling, that by making a movie you could totally replicate what was inside your head.

Something was bothering me. Was it the idea of happiness, was it desire? I didn't know what it was. To try and find out, you approach it from various angles. Was it an absence? Was there a center? All that remains are approaches, signs read from animal droppings, hitting a wall. What would be vivid? An afternoon, a bicycle basket, some faraway music, the back of a cab. Certain occurrences stood out in my mind, I couldn't wake up.

The edits became a very high form of mental drift. It was a way of turning your own confusion, your small unhappiness, into something magnificent. A

garde/innovative poetry is a series of located and specific scenes, each with their own concerns, rather than one unified scene. It argues, not only for U.S. poetry,

ho's" while the real cultural work goes ignored and undone. In our cruel society, all humanitarian progress attributable to America's social movements at the end of the 20th century, including feminism, has been successfully neutralized or reversed by fierce, greed-driven economic forces, be they corporate or entrepreneurial. Our notion of democracy is a myth politicians perpetuate to sustain our superiority among the nations of the world. Instead of an equitable democratic republic, in which women and others are fairly represented, and are able to seek their own socio-economic level without deleterious interference, we have, instead, a paper democracy, one existing only in those ideals expressed on the parchment of the Constitution of the United States.

•

Q - "how much you have in your wallet?"
A - to paraphrase an old African-American saying, "enough green to cover one's gender."

---

very do-it-yourself epistemology. The edits were highly manipulative. As girls, they say, always are.

The film remains inconclusive.

Works Cited:

Gilles Deleuze & Claire Parnet. *Dialogues*. New York: Columbia University Press, 1987.
Kathy Acker. *Blood & Guts in High School*. New York: Grove Press, 1984.
Ariana Reines. *The Cow*. New York: Fence Books, 2006.

but for U.S. poetries. Like many anthologies of its time, it is famous for its lack of attention to writing by women. It has 44 men and 4 women (or 8% women).

Gender Trouble
Juliana Spahr

I went to graduate school from 1989-1995 in Buffalo. So a lot of my vision of the '90s is limited and defined by this experience. It was cold in Buffalo about 8 months of the year and so I and some of my female colleagues often wore under the short slightly flouncy skirts that were popular at that time either thick, dark tights or tight-fitting long underwear and then usually some sort of boot, not the kind with heels that are popular today but the more practical kind commonly used in our culture for tromping around in snow, a Doc Marten sort of boot or a combat boot. I usually combined this with some girly top, like maybe a cut off slip or some sort of camisole that I bought at Victoria's Secret in the mall, and then as many thrift store sweaters as were necessary to stay warm—often a pull over and then an oversized cardigan on top of this.

What I am saying is that the performance of gender that Butler so astutely describes in *Gender Trouble* didn't feel like it got at how I performed gender as much as the cold performed gender for me. Buffalo was a cold place with a

---

from *Red Parts*
Maggie Nelson

from **"An Inheritance"**

If you were to ask my mother a few years ago how Jane's murder affected the upbringing of her two daughters, she would have said that it did not. In a television interview that she and I eventually granted to a show from CBS, *48 Hours Mystery*, during Leiterman's trial, my mother told the attractive, busty interviewer that she thought she had always been too "in control" to allow her sister's death to affect her behavior in any substantive way. The realization that she may not have been as "in control" as she imagined—a realization delivered, in part, by reading *Jane*, which chronicles the many years she spent barricading doors, etc.—startled her.

My mother remains equally startled by the fact that her body gets hungry, has to go to the bathroom, or reacts to environmental factors such as altitude or temperature. She dreams of an impermeable, self-sufficient body, one not subject

And it was not alone. Paris Leary and Robert Kelly's *A Controversy of Poets* (1965) has 51 men and 8 women (or 14%). Ron Padgett and David Shapiro's

heroic male literary tradition. And as graduate students we met in various bars late at night, after we had done some reading and some writing alone in our large yet cold rented apartments, and talked about things like radical modernism. And legacies. And male poets. We talked not reflectively about male poets as MALE poets, but just compulsively about male poets as if we were not even noticing that we just talked about male poets. We couldn't help ourselves. The heroic male literary tradition felt as if it was a warm breeze in the middle of a cold Buffalo winter. A warmth that maybe came from the ghosts of the living and the dead, the warm breath left behind by Charles Olson and Al Cook, and Michael Davidson and Jack Clarke and Gregory Corso and John Weiners and Robert Haas and Charles Altieri and Steven Rodefer and Albert Glover merged in our minds with the heroic myths the city told about itself, such as that it wasn't for pussies because it dealt with the cold and snow more than most other places in the nation.

Every year a fresh new group of students would arrive to join the English Department. Every year the admissions committee would have admitted a woman or maybe two who said in their application that they were interested

---

to uncontrollable needs or desires, be they its own or those of others. She dreams of a body that cannot be injured, violated, or sickened unless it chooses to be.

Recently, my mother tripped while speaking to my sister Emily on the phone. She fell to the floor in her kitchen, and her tooth smashed up against her upper lip. Her lip was swollen beyond recognition for weeks, and the tooth died; eventually she had to have a root canal. On the phone, my sister had no idea that she had fallen, because our mother talked right through it. When Emily and I bug her about this cover-up after the fact, she protests, *What purpose could it possibly have served to tell Emily that I'd had an accident? She couldn't have helped me, and it only would have made her worry.*

She says the fall was too embarrassing to mention. I say that it might have been worth mentioning simply because it happened. We may as well be talking to each other from opposite ends of a cardboard tube.

By the time my mother and I find ourselves at the *48 Hours* interview, seated side by side in a wainscoted room at the U of M Law School that CBS has taken over for the shoot and lined with fruit, coffee, and cookies, it is the last day of Leiterman's trial, and we will have spent weeks looking at autopsy photos of Jane

Anthology of New York Poets **(1970), has 26 men and 1 woman (or 4% women). And in his introduction to** ***The San Francisco Poets*** **(1971), with 6 men and no**

in studying twentieth century poetry. Every year, by the second semester, this woman or two would have changed the focus of her or their study.

But in contrast, the study of poetry of the male heroic literary tradition that used fragmentation, quotation, disruption, disjunction, agrammatical syntax, and so on seemed to be a magnet for men. Men would enter the program planning to do the muckraking, hard hitting masculinist American literature dissertation that Buffalo was so famous for. Leslie Fiedler—a cult academic because of both his arrest for possession of pot in the 70s and his "Come Back to the Raft Ag'in, Huck Honey" article that looked at the raft of Huck and Jim as a homosocial space—drew them to the program. But once they got there they would quickly decide to write a dissertation on the early works of a male poet who used fragmentation, quotation, disruption, disjunction, agrammatical syntax, and so on; the field is wide open, they would exclaim; there has been no full length study on the early works of this poet.

Those of us who studied the poetry of fragmentation, quotation, disruption, disjunction, agrammatical syntax, and so on were a group, a herd, and we were well known for building networks of burrows. We went to parties together.

---

projected on a big screen in the courtroom. I will have started to understand where my mother's fantasy of a sovereign, impermeable self might have come from.

A medical examiner had described each of these photos out loud at the January hearing. There was no jury then, and thus no need for projected pictures. As the examiner spoke, tears streamed involuntarily from my eyes, from my sister's eyes. But my mother did not cry. Her body simply collapsed in on itself. Her shoulders rounded over, her chest hollowed out, her whole body becoming more and more of a husk. Her knees shaking in spasms. I wanted to touch her but I didn't know what kind of touch would help. First I tried pressing my hands down lightly on the top of her shaking thighs, then I put a hand to her back. She did not respond to either. It was clear that she had entered a world beyond touch, a world beyond comfort.

My sister and I escaped to the bathroom at a break, and there Emily told me that she could barely look at our mother. She simply could not bear to see her in so much pain. I agreed, but did not confess to the less-admirable emotion. I also felt angry. I wanted our mother to meet these details with squared shoulders. I couldn't bear the way this man's words were shrivelling her body into that of a

women at all, David Meltzer casually claims, "The six poets in this book represent the history of poetry in San Francisco, in America, in the world." //

We sat near each other in seminars. We went to the same bars at night. But despite our collective investment in the male heroic tradition, we divided ourselves uneasily into buck rabbits, doe rabbits, jack-kit bunnies, and jill-kit bunnies because of the heroic male literary tradition. It was as if the male heroic literary tradition demanded such a division and we agreed to it because we couldn't see our way out of it; we couldn't hold on to the heroic male literary tradition if we didn't give in to these divisions.

The divisions were larger than all of us. They were structural. Among ourselves, talking to each other in the bar, it was hard for us to tell who was a jack-kit bunny and who was a jill-kit bunny beneath all the thrift store sweaters. We kept our sex organs inside our clothing and to identify which of us was which, someone had to hold us upside down so as to hypnotize us and then use their forefinger and middle finger to press down the vent area just in front of our anus so as to make our sex organs protrude. If we were a jill-kit bunny, we would then display a slit and a central line running up and down each side of our slit would be banded in pink. If we were a jack-kit bunny, there would be a blunt white tube without a central line that looked like a bullet. Because we were bunnies, and not rabbits, someone had to look very closely to see the difference.

---

little girl. I didn't want her to turn away; I didn't want her to shake. As I watched my beautiful sister wash and dry her hands and apply lipstick I tried to imagine how I'd feel if I were looking at autopsy photos of her on a big screen instead of Jane; the thought brought a quick flash of guilt and paralysis, followed by a wave of nausea. This was my mother's sister. What was I expecting?

You never saw such a wild thing as my mother, her hat seized by the winds and blown out to sea so that her hair was her white mane, her black lisle legs exposed to the thigh, her skirts tucked round her waist, one hand on the reins of the rearing horse while the other clasped my father's service revolver and, behind her, the breakers of the savage, indifferent sea, like the witnesses of a furious justice, writes Angela Carter in her retelling of the Bluebeard myth.

In Carter's version of the story, Bluebeard does not murder his young bride. Instead her mother arrives in the nick of time and puts "a single, irreproachable bullet" through Bluebeard's head.

Is this what I was hoping for?

Parallel to these anthologies, as Ashton points out, a number of anthologies by women are published as a corrective to this sort of editing. Among those that

But it was easier to tell who was a buck rabbit and who a doe rabbit. Only the buck rabbits—there were five of them—had endowed chairs with budget lines for travel and to bring people to the university to read and dole out to graduate student projects as they saw fit. The one doe rabbit affiliated with the Poetics Program did not have such a line. This was all the more noticeable because the doe rabbit was actually better known and more established than some of the buck rabbits. And this was called a "shame" and "an accident of hiring" by the buck rabbits and was blamed on the English Department's hiring practices, not the heroic male literary tradition that built its burrows.

This division, this gender trouble, was both profound and mundane but it shaped all of us into a pattern that we could not control. While most of us would say we were feminists—buck rabbits and jack kit rabbits included—the heroic male literary tradition had set up a complicated apparatus that supported the blunt white tube over the slit banded in pink that none of us could escape. For instance, there were two sorts of funding lines for graduate students. One, the one most jack-kit bunnies and jill-kit bunnies got, involved teaching two courses a year. Then there was another that involved nothing more than doing errands,

---

from "The Face of Evil"

He has come to gas the house and I am chained into a large birdcage that clangs against everything when I walk around. I'm trying to get up the stairs in the cage but it's hard. He acted very affectionate and kind when he came to gas the house and yet I knew he was going to kill me. Clearly he is deranged. I clang my way out of the house, noticing that he has duct-taped all the vents, etc. I burst out onto a lawn which sloped down into mud, toward a river. The mud feels amazingly green and wet and good, very real. I know instantly that the mud is the savior, the mud is the antidote to the poison gas. Later when he comes back he tries to act unsurprised that I am still alive, but he is obviously quite surprised. I hog-tie him and put him in a black garbage bag and go to burn him alive. I am thinking, I know this is only a dream, but am I really going to let myself do all these aggressive and violent things? I muse for a moment on how heavy the bag will probably be because he is such a big guy, but being a dream it doesn't give me any problem. Once he is tied up and in the bag, he doesn't make any noise anymore, it's like he's ceased to exist.

Ashton mentions are *No More Masks! An Anthology of Poems by Women* (1973), *Rising Tides: 20th Century American Women Poets* (1973), *Psyche: The Feminine*

like picking up poets at the airport for a buck rabbit and this line paid more than the teaching lines. Probably because the buck rabbits felt the most comfortable with jack-kit bunnies as their assistants, they gave their lines exclusively to jack-kit bunnies. When the jill-kit bunnies complained because they couldn't even apply to be rejected from the lines, one of the buck rabbits said that because the jill-kit bunnies were so devoted to teaching and the jack-kit bunnies did such a bad job of it, that it made more sense for the jack-kit bunnies to run the errands and be paid more.

This is just one example of the complicated financing system that the heroic male literary tradition left behind. I don't know how to describe it without insane amounts of detail and minutia. In retrospect, I am also struck by the small amounts of money we are talking about and how pathologically we analyzed the distribution spread. The buck rabbits gave out lines that paid $10,000 a year. The department gave out lines that paid $8,000 a year. And the rare books collection gave out jobs by the hour at a little over minimum wage. You might be able to imagine the gender spread in those jobs. But you might find it incomprehensible to imagine how seriously we took the small differences in such small amounts

---

And so I have dreamt for years of confronting some sinister, composite epitome of male violence and power, the murderer I always presumed to be Jane's. Sometimes he is a faceless shadow; other times he has the face of someone I know. Sometimes my mother and sister are there, and we help each other. Other times we are all there but we don't help each other, either because we can't or we won't. Most often I am alone.

My only other image of Jane's potential murderer was that of John Collins, who, at the time of his arrest, was a young, handsome white boy, and apparently quite the charmer. *Lucky with the ladies,* as they say.

Holding hands, sitting side by side on our bench at the January hearing, my mother, Emily, and I now watch an overweight, bespectacled, sixty-two-year-old man in a forest-green prison jumpsuit shuffle into the courtroom. He is mostly bald, with white, craggy hair in a crescent shape, and a face full of whiskers, which he runs his hands over frequently. He has a large, bulbous nose that occasionally flushes dark red, and small, stunned eyes. Under the defense table, his feet lie flat against the floor, shackled at the ankles, in black socks and plastic brown prison

Poetic Consciousness (1973), and the *Penguin Book of Women Poets* (1978). What is most striking is how little overlap there is between these feminist

of pay. How they built and tore down our self esteem. How they angered and pacified us. I imagine that these differences were incomprehensible to the rabbits at the time also, that the differences were so small that only bunnies with their limited eye sight could chart them.

Basically, we were all stuck together in this burrow none of us dug. It was not that the doe rabbit and the jill-kit bunnies were innocent. We were stuck together in this burrow with narrow mud walls that had been dug out before we got there. It was hard for us to figure out where to dig to expand the burrow or how to make new openings into it because we had not created it. As doe rabbits and jill-kit bunnies, we were experienced with closing down openings to the burrow in order to protect the young, not with building new openings. We too were caught. We stupidly used essentialism as an epithet and tossed it at each other. We had troubles building things together. When one of us complained about gender stuff, another of us shot her observations down. We couldn't see our way into the things that get talked about in *Gender Trouble*, a book which we could have read as a how-to guide on escaping or reclaiming the heroic male literary tradition. While the jack-kit bunnies circulated petitions to the admissions committee saying that they should admit various jack-kit bunnies

---

sandals. Periodically he takes off his glasses and cleans them with the edge of his green prison shirt, then squints back out at the courtroom. The few times he turns around to scan the entire room he looks completely disoriented, as if he has no idea where he is.

I feel disoriented too. Where I imagined I might find the "face of evil," I am finding the face of Elmer Fudd.

On this day Leiterman spends a lot of time watching his hands, which for the most part stay in a steepled position in front of his face or against his swollen belly. I am reminded of his nursing career by the way he shoots into action when anyone in the courtroom needs to put on latex gloves to handle evidence. Otherwise fairly motionless, he quickly picks up the box of powdered gloves and shakes it out to witnesses or lawyers whenever they need them, often a moment before the need arises, with a nurse's instinct for protection. In the late afternoon a deep shaft of sunlight moves over the courtroom, and eventually lands on the defense table. Everyone else shifts positions or moves seats to get out of it, but Leiterman cannot move, he has to abide it. I watch the sun saturate his face and body, watch him shield his face with his hands in vain. Just as he instinctively

anthologies and the experimental/postmodern/avant-garde/innovative anthologies. The women included in the latter anthologies tend not to appear in the former

to the English Department, the jill-kit bunnies, including myself, signed them and we did not bother to circulate petitions of our own, choosing instead to mumble when the jack-kit bunny showed up about there being too many jack-kit bunnies. When the doe rabbit was given a budget by the buck rabbits, she didn't bring in any doe rabbit or jill-kit bunnies to read, she used the money to show all of the films of Chris Marker. And I distinctly remember a buck rabbit telling me that Kevin Killian was complaining to him that there were not any queers invited to the New Coast conference and replying that I didn't know the sexuality of most of the people invited and the buck rabbit saying, pointedly and justly, that is probably his point.

At moments we managed to form smallish groups of jill-kit bunnies and get things. Although I can't prove it with a memory of conversation, I'm sure one of the reasons two of us included only doe rabbits and jill-kit bunnies in the first issue of a journal we started was that we felt we could get guilt money from the buck rabbits. And once when the doe rabbit was going on leave, we jill-kit bunnies had a meeting and wrote a letter to the chair saying that we didn't want the doe rabbit replaced with another buck rabbit who used fragmentation, quotation, disruption, disjunction, agrammatical syntax, and so on in his writing;

---

offers up the gloves, I feel the urge to shield him, to block the sun with my body, or at least put down a shade.

We stay planted in our positions; I watch the light move over him.

I watch the light and I watch his hands and I try to imagine them around the trigger of a gun, I try to imagine them strangling someone. Strangling Jane. I know this kind of imagining is useless and awful. I wonder how I'd feel if I imagined it over and over again and later found out that he didn't do it. I stare at him all day as if a sign were about to come down from the heavens to indicate his guilt or innocence. It doesn't come.

until 1974 when Kelsey Street Press begins publishing. There is, as many have pointed out, a skepticism in the experimental/postmodern/avant-garde/

we felt it was crucial to hire a doe rabbit. The chair complied and a doe rabbit came and this was a good thing but our success felt somewhat lessened because most of the jack-kit bunnies refused to take her classes; the classes she offered were not interesting to them, they explained.

The anger that this remark provoked in at least one of us was almost pathological. It was the anger of suddenly realizing gender trouble. The anger of an anxiety that all those jill-kit bunnies who said in their applications that they were interested in studying twentieth century poetry who then changed their focus of study were right. The anger that arose when the buck rabbit who ran the rare book collection called the jill-kit bunnies secretaries; bring your secretary he would say to the jack-kit bunnies when they set up meetings. I don't know how to describe this anger. But I think I attempted to when writing "Thrashing Seems Crazy," a poem that felt overwrought when I wrote it and I never understood why I wrote it. And it feels even more overwrought now. But I did not connect this overwrought-ness to various events until I started writing this piece. I have for years instead only noticed how it was from *Oprah* and how it seemed a certain weird and yet literal example of some of the ideas in *Gender Trouble*.

To speak the true saga of desire—not the action driven capture of an object one—rather, the relentless and perpetual story of all creativity and being.
Timeless and dark and spatial and repetitive as waves.

The what if story were repetition.

The what if story were fragments strung together as a life.

The what if of a story dipping in and out of myth, epic, identity, spatiality.

innovative scene to embrace feminism and/or publishing projects limited to women. // By the '80s, this does change a little and a whole series of "feminist

Embracing Form: Pedagogical Sketches of Black Women Students Influenced by Hip Hop
Tracie Morris

Parallels of growth

We are often teaching to aspects of our selves, sometimes simply our younger selves and other times repudiations of former selves. In my earlier iterations as a poet, I was known as a Hip Hop poet and, in the early '90s, was somewhat rare as a woman engaging that style at the time. Hip Hop poetry, like Hip Hop itself, mirrored the gender emphasis at the time. What this focus contrasts with however, is the preponderance of women in poetry classes. Where does this leave the young black women whose generation and cultural references are defined by Hip Hop, but who explicitly chose poetry as their medium of expression?

I have seen two ways in which young Black women work artistically in this territory: their texts emphasize politics in general and Black cultural nationalism in particular (sometimes feminist-affirming, sometimes not), and romantic relationships, particularly relationships that express longing. In other words,

---

In Praise of the Anti-Social
Maggie Nelson

Editor's Note: This paper was given in response to the question: can women's writing change the social imaginary?

The social—i.e., what we're doing here today—is rich with possibilities. Nonetheless, I'm going to focus on the no-obligations, non-strategic, essentially solitary space that I feel so much writing takes place in, to see if I can articulate how and why I think this space plays a crucial role in relation to "the social."

One can, and often must, utilize all sorts of strategies in one's writing—to start it, to direct it, to structure it, to keep going with it, etc. But strategy often seems clearest in retrospect, at which time one can talk about it coherently, as if one had been following guideposts all along, when in fact the road may have been no road at all, but rather a complete disintegration of strategy or ethos. So I guess I've become interested, by necessity, in that disintegration, the navel of strategy, strategy's blindspots, the painful times and places at which it leaves you

interventions" happen. *Raddle Moon* **and** *How(ever)* **begin in 1983. In 1984,** *Poetics Journal* **publishes an issue on "Women and Language." In 1989, Dodie**

though these young women often position themselves in conventional black female roles in their work, they add to this the assertive phrasings inherent in Hip Hop rhyme.

If young men, irrespective of nationality, engage Hip Hop as rhyme reference for their creative texts—with nuances that suggest inspiration from many popular performers—who are young Black women inspired by in the Hip Hop era and in what ways do they employ rhyme? To explore these questions, I consider the use of rhyme by a number of contemporary women performers who are both influenced by Hip Hop aesthetics, and who engage in Hip Hop inflected performances.

•

One of the earliest references to poetry explicitly in rhymed performance is in MC Lyte's "Lyte as a Rock," where, after opening with the phrase, "I am the lyte a-a-a-a-a-a-as-as-a-rock l-y, l-l-y-t-e," the performer goes on to ask the question, "Do you understand the metaphoric phrase, lyte as a rock?" Lyte's voicing, particularly her low-range "masculine" sounding voice, establishes her authority as an MC, while the rhyme scheme she uses is conventional aabb.

---

naked in the woods. When something you thought was going to be a feminist battle-cry turns into something hopeless, or vice versa. When you find you have to give up on wisdom, on empowerment, on "change for the better," and give into the force that cuts through any smugness you may have once had about knowing how things are or should be.

It's at this point that Fanny Howe's formulation—that the point of art is "to show people that life is worth living by showing that it isn't"—comes in. I think sometimes you have to give into the sentiment that another world isn't possible in order to believe that one is. You have to go through the looking glass. I'm not saying this is a pretty state. It might be what Francis Bacon meant when he talked about "exhilarated despair," a state I feel quite familiar with. But I won't go down that road now.

•

Instead I want to talk about two poets who've changed my "social imaginary," both of whom could be deemed either explicitly unconcerned about feminist strategy or devoted to it.

Bellamy edits a woman's only issue of *Mirage*, and *Big Allis* publishes only women in its first, and several subsequent issues. Also, as Ashton observes,

She also engages in the boasting motif typical of many male rappers. One of the most renowned and popular MCs from the early '90s, MC Lyte, known for her strong performative skills, has a contemporary in the late '90s-early 2000s in Lauryn Hill. Ms. Hill, a vocalist and rapper, is representative of a tendency of progressive Black women performers influenced by Hip Hop who use a "song" voice in conjunction with a "recitation" voice. By recitation voice I mean the conventional (and often deliberately performative) voice for speaking words into a microphone. The song voice is that which is by its nature performative through the singing of sounds. Song has long been a vehicle for encoded language in the African American community, as it has been for many others. What is striking however is how frequently Hip Hop influenced women use the song voice as well as recitation voice, which is the general mode of Hip Hop influenced work. Most women who rap also sing on their albums or on subsequent releases. Why is this? What is compelling women who rhyme to be singers, too?

•

While becoming a "singing sister" allows for a more fully corporeal engagement with text by the performer, for "hard core" Hip Hop enthusiasts this can be

---

The first is unfashionable: I want to say a few words about Sylvia Plath. Plath was the first poet who inspired me not only to become a writer, but also to become a feminist. In high school I had felt extremely empowered by Plath—in particular, by the quality of her line, which felt to me like nothing less than a razor cutting through veils of delusion and pabulum, and by her use of consonance, which was so electric and over-the-top—so wicked, so campy, so irresponsible—I simply couldn't believe that she got away with it. "Its snaky acids kiss./It petrifies the will. There are the isolate, slow faults/That kill, that kill, that kill." When I look back at the writers that most affected my own way of working, I see Plath's clarity of line and sound—along with her willingness to be completely unlikable—animal, even (a true "bitch," as she has so often been called)—that led me to whatever clarity and bravery I've found since. Later I looked for, and found, these traits in a number of other women writers: Susan Sontag, Joan Didion, Lydia Davis, Lucille Clifton, Jane Bowles, Simone Weil, Ivy Compton-Burnett, Claudia Rankine, Anne Carson, and so on. Of course I admire many other writers. But I'm trying to isolate a kind of caustic lucidity here—a certain ability to cut through cant, moral obtuseness, and bullshit of all stripes—which I associate with feminist consciousness, good art-making, and activism.

there are some changes in the numerical representation of women's writing in '80s experimental/postmodern/avant-garde/innovative anthologies. Both Donald

jarring, even disappointing sometimes as many fans wish that these rare female voices in hip hop would focus on the "devastating rhymes" that establish their careers. MC Lyte, Queen Latifah, and particularly Lauryn Hill are all examples. Lauryn Hill, considered one of the best MC's in Hip Hop irrespective of gender, is considered a particularly sad "loss" to song, even though she, like her sisters, are good singers.

In Hip Hop almost every early woman rapper who is well-known eventually incorporates singing into her repertoire. My contention is that for young female Hip Hop influenced writers, the song voice serves a similar purpose as do the themes of love: it allows them to better fit the conventions that frame the acceptable role of the Black female utterance in established culture.

Besides the cultural support that reinforces strong Black female vocal tradition, I have often wondered why women rappers become singers. In Queen Latifah's case, it was a savvy career choice. As she focused on her acting career she was less and less concerned with keeping up with the fresh nuances and sonic collaborations of novel Hip Hop trends. She's a good singer, is not a "kid" anymore and segued from one vocal framework to another. Lyte and Hill,

---

•

Imagine my surprise, then, when in my first year of college, I picked up a book by a feminist critic titled *Art and Anger: Reading like a Woman*, and read the following pronouncement: "Plath was not a feminist; her novels and poems are not feminist. [...] She offers no solutions except Hedda Gabler's. Gas ovens for mothers' daughters, guns for fathers' daughters; neither are weapons which help us make ourselves into our own women. [...] May her nets and hooks soon be in a mausoleum of memory of what a dependent woman's pain and anger looked like, and Plath's name on the wall as its best recorder." Plath had helped me to become "my own woman"; did that mean something was wrong with me? And why would any woman want to embalm and imprison another in a mausoleum? Reading this, I felt about as ashamed as I felt when I first read feminist savagings of Henry Miller and *Story of O*—my two much beloved stand-bys for getting off on. Talk about feeling accused of false consciousness.

In retrospect I'm not sorry for any of these confusions—allowing yourself to be turned on and off by the same sources, finding feminist roots in places that

Allen and George Butterick's 1982 revision of *New American Poetry* **called** *The Postmoderns: The New American Poetry Revisited* **and Ron Silliman's 1983** *In*

however, did not make these shifts based on the same considerations as Latifah. I believe that there is a subtext of pressure for these women to demonstrate identity *as voice*. My perspective on this is not only based upon the use of song by popular Black women rappers but also by singers who've been influenced by rap, particularly neo-soul singers who convey their personas through Hip Hop and song in a way that is considered "pro-black." Three examples I'd like to briefly consider here to compliment the three rappers previously discussed are Mary J. Blige, Jill Scott and Erykah Badu, artists who also focus on relationships in a community-oriented way.

Blige is considered a woman who "keeps it real" and whose voice conveys honesty, pain and, ultimately in her particular case, self-empowerment. Blige has created an alter-ego rap character, Brooke Lynn, who has been featured on Blige's most recent recording and others. Erykah Badu and Jill Scott are also affiliated, as Scott is a songwriter who has written work used by Badu. Scott can also be seen as a more "afrocentric" presentation of the type of everyday urban aesthetic that catapulted Blige's persona. Badu is the most "afrocentrically-presented" of the three. She wears African inspired clothing and presents pan-african

---

other feminists deem terrible influences, loving the word "strategy" then feeling the urge to dump it in the nearest trash bin, wanting to make work that changes things "for the better," then just not giving a shit about any such thing—in my view these are contradictions that we not only deserve to live with, but are lucky to live with.

•

The second poet I want to mention is Alice Notley. Unlike Plath (who Notley decided early on was "a genuinely negative influence"), Notley has explicitly aimed to amplify—if not explode—the possibilities and contours of the social imaginary for decades—what kinds of worlds can be thought, imagined, and articulated. As she once put it in a talk on women poets and the epic at Naropa, "We don't need new words, new languages, new syntax; we need a whole new flesh, new beings to look at, literally, a new universe. The key is not in language, but in vision." Notley's epics—*The Descent of Alette* in particular—often seem governed—or at least initiated—by a dogged employment of feminist strategy and obligation. But as soon as you get submerged in them, you find yourself in a soup of untamed, non-strategic, anarchic poetry. I'm thinking, for example,

the American Tree, have 31% women. Bruce Andrews' and Charles Bernstein's 1984 *The L=A=N=G=U=A=G=E Book* has 56 men and 13 women (or 19%

aesthetics in her visual imagery. In song and image all these women underscore a community commitment, an unequivocally pro-black presentation that defines their femaleness. The students in my classes frequently reference these women as role models in their work aesthetically and in their own visual presentations. My argument is that the incorporation of song into the repertoire of the Black woman rapper concretizes her gender as clearly as a hairstyle, clothing mode or overt political statement. In other words, dominant conventions of Black womanhood for performers demand that this be not only recited, but also voiced.

•

Sound pedagogy
Having recognized the importance and place of song, we can now ask how these elements affect pedagogical approaches, particularly those that emphasize form and editing for young Black women who engage in poetics with song and rap as a base? First I'd like to discuss the type of writing I'm coming across and how that intersects with what I like to teach. Then I'd like to talk about these students' work and shifts in tone and usage with exposure to "conventional" poetry, and how this challenges the conventions of voiced Black womanhood.

---

of Part One of *Alette*, in which Alette descends into the nightmarish, surreal maze of subways which eventually takes her to the center of the world, and to her eventual confrontation with "the Tyrant" who has hijacked it. At one point Alette sees an eyeball scurrying across the floor of a subway car, and remarks: "This eyeball's funny" "on the gray floor"/"among round stains" "& ashes" . . . "I guess it's blue-eyed" "dark blue" "No eyebrows, of / course" "Doesn't blink much" "Intent" "intent on looking"/ "What's it looking for?" "I guess, whatever." The focus here is on imagining, and on looking carefully at one's imaginings, even if the scrutiny must end in mystification or indifference: "I guess, whatever."

•

I admire this strategic/non-strategic mess of Notley's monster poems very much, which I suspect stems from something Notley calls a "poetics of disobedience," i.e., her "rejection of everything [she] was supposed to be or affirm, all the poetries all the groups the clothes the gangs the governments the feelings and reasons." She goes on to say that while writing her 2001 epic *Disobedience*, she discovered that she could not go along "with the government or governments, with radicals and

women). Douglas Messerli's 1987 *"Language" Poetries* includes 13 men and 6 women (or 32% women). // By the 1990s, an editor of an anthology would find

The students who are attracted to my performance poetry classes have emerged from the so-called "spoken word" movement that developed in the mid-90's and has been subsequently publicized through MTV, poetry-on-tour and other outlets. In mass media culture, poetry is a subset of popular song, not an entity with a much older precedent.

These young women see performance poetry as a mode through which they can be confrontational and vocal in their expressions. They get to "talk back". With the exception of the more cloistered art school setting, most undergraduate women in mixed gender classrooms tend to express themselves in the passive voice. The poetry slams, cafés and other venues encourage their speaking outside the confines of the class. When they sign up for a performance poetry class, then, they often have experience speaking aloud and seek affirmation regarding their aesthetic and ultimately feminist choice (even if it is not defined in these terms). They are looking for support from me, not generally in terms of writing, but in terms of performing for credit and performing better.

•

---

certainly not with conservatives or centrists, with radical poetics, and certainly not with other poetics, with other women's feminisms, with any fucking thing at all; belonging to any of it was not only an infringement on [her] liberty but a veil over clear thinking."

Notley's "fuck you" attitude—which she freely extends out to her readers—is a far cry from writing under any obligation to effect or affect the social imaginary in positive ways. And for the record, Notley often says that she despises formulations involving the words "we" or "our." But, of course, bringing about transformative change in the psyches of her readers—or radically expanding their sense of what forms of life or organization are possible—is precisely what Notley's epics do—or, at least, what they have done for me.

•

Perhaps this is a strange place to end up, in an essay about feminism and "the social"—lauding one writer who is a notoriously "bad" influence, and another who has made some of the most anti-social comments I can think of. Notley has even gone so far as to say, "I think of myself as disobeying my readership a lot. I began

it almost impossible to argue that writing by women wasn't visible or wasn't part of the experimental scene. A huge number of feminist interventions happen

Teaching these students is challenging because of the particular constraints of the medium that inspired them. Rappers/Rhymers, the vocalists of Hip Hop, are primarily writers but not solely so. They (or the producer) also work with musical sounds that often encourage literary choices and devices that aren't specific to writing well-crafted texts that stand on their own. Furthermore, Black women students influenced by rap have the added constraint of working with forms of Hip Hop that also explicitly employ song. The musicality inherent in spoken word, such as modulation, embellishment and alliteration, are often 'hedged" (as 'risky' ventures often are) by the constraints of conforming to the acceptable norms of the "sung-Black-woman's" vocal. All these aspects of voicing involve thinking about how words work as music, not solely on their own terms. It can be very disorienting for these students to have to start at square one as "just" writers, i.e., artists using words disengaged from music and performance. For all students, this can be a difficult experience but for those whose sense of a writerly self is at once strongly reinforced and fragile, it is confusing and is often interpreted, initially, as a rejection of their deeply held cultural influence on the sonic and performative qualities of words.

---

the new work denying their existence." Can denying the existence of a readership be precisely the means by which a significant social bond between reader and writer is created? I think so—by virtue of the same logic, which maintains that one can come to feel that life is worth living via a fearless exposition of why it is not. For when it comes to reading and writing—experiences which I would differentiate, by virtue of their claims on solitude and duration, from taking in visual spectacle or participating in social or political events—an embrace of the perverse, the hopeless, the non-strategic, the non-utilitarian, and the antisocial, can often be the unlikely means by which we gain a visceral sense of our shared condition, and by which we find the guts to transform what we find most odious and unjust in it.

Works Cited:

Fanny Howe. "Bewilderment." *The Wedding Dress*. Berkeley: University of California Press, 2003.
Jane Marcus. *Reading like a Woman*. Columbus: The Ohio State University Press, 1988.
Alice Notley. "Epic and Women Poets." *Disembodied Poetics*. Albuquerque: University of New Mexico Press, 1994.
Alice Notley. *The Descent of Alette*. New York London: Penguin, 1992.
Sylvia Plath. "Elm." *The Collected Poems*. New York: Harper & Row, 1981.

in the '90s, including: Rachel Blau DuPlessis's now iconic critical study on women writers and experimentalism, *The Pink Guitar*; the journal *Chain*, by

I try to take care with this sense of vulnerability but my primary concern is that the students write strong texts that can stand on the page irrespective of the power of performance. This is critical because I do see these women as strong writers and am afraid for them: that without attention to craft they will feel good about themselves in my course, but that when they leave they will be more vulnerable to the biases of editors, teachers and reviewers who use their lack of experience in the craft of poetry as an excuse to reject them completely. Many of us as women, people of color, people who are of marginalized populations, know this technique: the so-called objective criticism that rationalizes identity-based discrimination. I, like most of you, I'm sure, have faced this phenomenon in the various undergraduate and graduate settings that we experienced as students.

•

So these wonderful black women, their classmates and I, start over together, and in this starting from "square one" it is critical to affirm their voices and *only* talk shop about the poetic effectiveness in terms of craft. One has to consciously and routinely separate what they are saying with how they are trying to say it and to

---

Chapter Seven, or, I Do What I Don't Want To Do
Stephanie Young

You shouldn't have any trouble understanding this, friends,
the idea of society *is* a powerful image
for you know, know ye not, or are ye ignorant, brethren,
in the beginning was emotion…
Do you not know, brothers, I speak,
potent in its own right
I am speaking to them, men who know
Celine often repeated in his writings and interviews
the law, all the ins and outs the law hath,
this image has form
how that has authority over a man, dominion
reading him, one has the impression
how it works, and how its power only touches the living
that in the beginning was discomfort

Jena Osman and Spahr; O'Sullivan's *Out of Everywhere*; *Outlet*, edited by Elizabeth Treadwell and Sarah Anne Cox; *Moving Borders*, Jordan Davis and

underscore their unique voice in each poem. That conceptual affirmation can be pulled apart from technical variances so they can be really *true* to their own voices through craft. Part of this effort to explore the voice is to expand it.

•

Craft specifics

I have found the most powerful tool for engaging students in the importance of both craft and culture is to analyze the scansion of poems; by this I mean the analysis of verse to highlight its specifically metrical qualities, amongst the many other sonic values in poetry. (This also helps in training the ear.) Scansion is the place where the two voices meet and, after much initial struggle, students feel confident about knowing a "poetry thing," a technical word, which can be applied to any poetic interpretation. They not only feel smarter on an intellectual level, they feel empowered by the way in which scansion illuminates the poetry they've written and thought they already knew. With Hip Hop, scansion cultivates an already more sensitized ear to the power, and pitfalls, of rhyme. We walk along the trajectory of rhyme and the various forms of it that are engaged for different effect in Hip Hop and in more conventionally canonical work.

---

as long as he lives
has external boundaries, margins, internal structure

For instance a wife
its outlines contain power to reward
the woman that has a husband
there is energy in its margins
bound by law
differentiated from chaos
but if he dies
this much is becoming known
if the husband be dead
for symbols
she is discharged
as incandescent, unbearable limit
So then if while the husband lives
no experience is too lowly
if she lives with another man

Chris Edgar's all women issue of *The Hat*; the webjournal *HOW2*, edited by Kate Fagan and others; and Yedda Morrison and David Buuck publish an issue

As we look at poetry more and more closely at this stage, the student usually becomes more frustrated with her work and tries to figure out what to do to make her poems "better," meaning both less obvious and simple in declaration and less overly reliant on the agreement of the political or cultural point of the line at the expense of making the reader, as well as the writer, care about it.

•

We then look closely at what images offer. I apply imagery in a limited way in my own work, which emphasizes sound, so I'm not operating here from my own aesthetic predilections. This surprises my students: I've found that what imagery offers pedagogically though, is an articulation of the words in a way that pulls the reader in. Hip Hop rhymes and the poetry influenced by them is full of filler words/placement terms (including plenty of indefinite articles, prepositions, conjunctions, etc.) that support the musicality of a stanza. It is challenging to suggest that the young Black female student move away from the music and focus on the words. This is sometimes interpreted as a cultural affront and I have found, for the reasons I alluded to earlier, it to be a challenge to ask

---

all in all, the most elaborate attempt
while her husband is living
she is called
how thresholds symbolize beginnings—
obviously she's an adulteress.
But if the husband die
his whole narrative stance seems uncontrolled
if her husband be dead
sighting the crest
though she be joined
why does the bridegroom carry his bride
She is quite free to marry
the step, the beam, the doorposts
with no one's disapproval.

Wherefore my brothers
you also died, were made dead
where sense topples

of *Tripwire* called "Gender" that pointedly includes a significant amount of work by women. In 1999, Rae Armantrout and Fanny Howe organize the

them to, even temporarily, trust the page over the ear. We work around that through example: I read the text of strong black writers, from Etheridge Knight and Lucille Clifton as well as really great rappers such as Biggie Smalls, LL Cool J (in his particular way) and Rakim Allah, to show them that there is no conflict in releasing the musical interpretation, temporarily, to use Pound's term, for the clarity of Phanopoesis.

One way to cultivate the writing voice that's different from their musical mode is to ask the students to write text outside of their conventional subject matter. I ask them, and all the students, to write oppositional characters and villains to shake up their preconceptions of what they are permitted to write. I ask them to modify their writing by analyzing the literary connotations of their own voices, using myself, and my somewhat grainy, mid-low range natural speaking voice as an example, then modifying that voice to let them hear the connotation voice has for their poems' meanings. They then apply different sounds to these non-personal characters. This combination of conceptual and physical voice shifting allows them to develop more options for their voices. In conjunction with these things I enforce and reinforce editing, removing the non-essential

---

to make a frame
through the body
which is a necessary everyday condition
that you might belong
entering a house
you might be joined
even to him
the way an animal is
free to marry
in half across the middle
bring forth fruit
for celebrating a truce
and this is something like what has taken place.

For when we were in
the flesh, excreta, breast milk, saliva
doing whatever we felt we could *get away with*

Pagemothers Conference at UCSD and that same year Rachel Levitsky begins the Belladonna reading series (current co-curator Erica Kaufman begins in

volume of words that are employed in Hip Hop for musical considerations and exploring the intense resonances of individual words. Often this is the most challenging part of pedagogy, stripping away the masks of prose so the poetics can unequivocally stand on its own in these powerful and newly "shaky" voices. By stepping away from the selves they know, the students write toward writing without feeling as if they're choosing sides.

•

The textual and sonic voices of these women create a complex relationship with self-identity. They see their female-ness defined by Blackness in specific ways in text and voice and I hope I give them some degree of support by offering technical suggestions for their work that expand and reinforce their aesthetics. In the classroom, the women with a pro-black stance are worried about being pushed away from the cultural moorings they know and rely on, because these senses of self help them get through racist and sexist institutional predispositions. This is largely due to the fact that when they are invalidated in school, often because of their lesser formal educational opportunities, they utilize this sense of pro-black identity as a protective wall. Their agency is questioned regularly. Their

---

a thin film
aroused by the law
constantly threatened with bursting
at work in our bodies
with maximal stylistic intensity.

But now
the narrative yields
we are delivered
used as a diagram
wherein we were held
two extremes that moreover change places
so that we can serve in a new way
because the rituals work upon human flesh
and not in the oldness of the letter.

But I can hear you say then
according to the most exact calculations

2002). // And yet, and alas, the anthology numbers are still far from Ashton's claim that by the mid-'80s efforts to redress the imbalance "had apparently

opinions are constantly deemed intellectually and culturally inferior by teachers and peers who have had more extensive formal educational opportunities. This phenomenon is well known to us here but for my students, (young Black female hip-hop inspired and hip-hop-performing poets), it is coupled with a new anxiety that they feel due to the appropriation by mass-culture of the gender and racial terms by which they identify their own specificity. They thus feel themselves in a paradoxical situation whereby, on the one hand, they feel their identities invalidated as not being "writerly," while on the other, their aesthetic is taken up and absorbed into the wider mass culture. Everyone is interested in Hip Hop now, everyone claims it: even "sensitive guys" claim feminism in the classroom on occasion. However, these guys are still ill-equipped, because of their own socialization, to relinquish domination of classroom discourse. The end result is that Hip Hop influenced women poets feel they are being cast as both lesser and redundant.

●

Breaking down the walls to let Black women write well means addressing race and identity as these dynamics play out in the classroom. It requires lovingly and

---

if it was no longer entirely part of herself
if the law-code was bad as all that
is the law sincerity?
Its own independent life?
Certainly not!
Here in town, the law-code has a perfectly legitimate function
on his estate I would not have known
what sincerity was
that far from needing pity
had not the law said
he was very attractive
I would not have known what coveting was.
His uncommonly expressive face
dressed up to look like a virtue
and timid politeness to women
ruined my life.
Don't you remember how it was

succeeded." // • Eliot Weinberger's 1993 *American Poetry Since 1950: Innovators and Outsiders* includes 30 men and 5 women (or 14% women). // • Messerli's

dispassionately critiquing the racial and gender dynamics that occur in class so the women and men of various backgrounds open up to free their voices, but not using those issues to critique the text of students. The confrontation and honesty in the classroom, even when the teacher comes across as a universal antagonist, in the opinion of all the students, helps them bond through language and the craft of writing even though they are different and each is struggling with her place in the world.

My reflections on pedagogy are a mirror of my own creative process, from journaling to hip hop poet to experimental writer and performer. The trajectory of my creative life has made me configure pedagogy not on a conventional MFA model but on one that takes into account the necessary autodidactism and cultural specificity that lets these women feel safe, write better and convey their own voices, to encourage them to appreciate the use of song and Hip Hop, to reincorporate it into their work, but to also help them place themselves in the world, to grow, fully flower as writers, to call themselves poets.

---

among the thousand things reflected there?
I do, perfectly well,
the place where that rose heap was on display
sincerity seized its opportunity
when I approached
found a way to pervert the command
which many another better man has
wrought in me
to handle and to smell
every kind of covetous desire
within a hedge
without all the paraphernalia of law—

compared to it, the perfume
sincerity looked pretty dull.

1994 *From the Other Side of the Century* includes 61 men and 19 women (or 24% women). // • Paul Hoover's 1994 *Postmodern American Poetry* includes 74 men

Four Poems
Susan McCabe

That Homer Girl

She packs poems like smelling salts so she can get to them in a crisis. She gave up saving money in a can under her mattress. Lost her workroom in a flood. She is so far into her mind she is out of it. Half-stars flicker on the hem of her changeable taffeta, the color of the sky under water. She reads fate in the filaments of iris. She's everyone's idea of a good time, the glass broken from the stem she dangles. When God poured the soul in, it was like water in water. They called her that Homer Girl, she danced the Odyssey with her body, Penelope at her belly, throwing the loom. We go back to where we begin no matter what. "I couldn't keep up with her café life, it was too fast," her girlfriend said. She smirks at the mustard mercedes

---

For I was alive apart from the law once
the year that followed was the saddest
but when the commandment came
sincerity sprang to life
and I was fooled.

And the commandment which was social
ordained unto impression management
intended to cooperate but
I found that discrepant roles developed.

For sincerity beguiled me
the library looked as she had pictured it
pretty much dead.

So then the law
had a fatalistic sense of itself

**and 27 women (or 27% women). // • Dennis Barone and Peter Ganick's 1994
The Art of Practice: 45 Contemporary Poets with 23 women and 22 men (or 51%**

and the drunken swaying ladies in it. Everything brings its shadow.
She tips her pocket periscope and almost drowns the boats on tour.
When she enters in her thistle coat, all clocks face away. She leaves
a little of her hair wet to dry in the wind. It's not enough just to know
it's there, the sea. Her bed-clothes streaming, she presses close to the
back of a mermaid biker. All of the night they ride. She tells them stories
while she sleeps; others believe they are dreaming them. Men become
swine if they forget her. Her feet sizzle. She sings to them. Her head
is a blue violin.

---

its good and common sense
being drawn from one wrong turning to another.
Did then that which is good become death?
Did the fact in itself still seem harmless enough?
Whose mind could be severely logical?
By no means.
They could be of use to each other
in order that sincerity
a fertile source of harmful complications
might become utterly sincere.

For we know that the law is spiritual
but I am carnal, dizziness, noises, buzzings, vomitings

for that which I do
on the rough seas of the English Channel
I do not understand

women) is the one exception we could find to the mixed gender anthology that includes more work by women than men. // • Leonard Schwartz, Joseph

Isis

I am the bride of bits and pieces.

Under a moon mostly lip,
how I necklaced myself in ditch and weed.

Yes, that was the hand that smoothed my forehead,
feathered it . . . even if I groped blind

in the love between blood and mud
to know you better that way, cut up—

Only one missing part no longer missing:
nibbled by mackerel, its bits now streaming,

a body beyond simple peg-and-hole joining,
hawk-head hunger of the stream-bed:

the lost thing doesn't always haunt.

---

and not only as a metaphor
what I want to do
and even more so the sick body
I do not do
what I don't understand
is that often I seem to be worn out

and if I do there is no glory
what I do not want to do
is best for myself and then do it

one of literature's most abominable scenes

it becomes obvious
the law is—
as it is
a buzzing pain that rises
in the same neutral tone.

Donahue, and Edward Foster's 1996 *Primary Trouble: An Anthology of Contemporary American Poetry* includes 41 men and 22 women (or 35% women).

Silver Axe in the Ninth

Daddy with brusque weather wisdom, clear-eyed under a children's
moon, racing form tattering in his coat. Smeared clarities loom.
Out of the welter they bubble.

Spill of cash and cloak and beer, red talk and cigarette pack,
behind-door fancy. Coming out of the tunnel they all look sainted.
Oh the many-colored striped, and the body curled into a spring.

This rickety summer with no-good weed ideas, horse friends floundering.
His pal McNealy's Ford Falcon speeds to make the first post, wife cringing
in the back. The track is a neo-Platonic truth. BELOVABLE in the third.

Even wet and murky, the turf spangled light. Swirl girl could pick
the winners: one with its blinders removed; the other with them added.
Wending her way between elbows, she crushes tickets beneath her.

I realize that in me
that is my flesh
omitted the phrenological head
I have the desire to do good:
plates, pots, chairs and lamps
but I cannot carry it out.

My decisions, such as they are
don't result in tightly fastened bootstraps.
Now if I do what I do not want to do
it is a vision
it is no longer I who do it
broken up by the rhythmic sound of the voice.
It is sincerity living in me
which prevents images from crystallizing
and gets the better of me every time
causing them to break out into sensation.

// • **Alan Kaufman and S. A. Griffin's 1999** *The Outlaw Bible of American Poetry* **includes 188 men and 57 women (or 23% women). // So what we ended up**

She will fill the pail of no thing to stroke the coat of THE HORSE.
Sling shot song in the dark along the mule mist. Carrying within
hole-y pockets—ah flower, ah ache.

She finds her hollow hideout after a pure crack across the face, the sky
(never matter) after SILVER AXE came in last. Oily horses unnerve him.
She slips insides into outsides, calico coats and the all-grey-one,
mane of kindling.

Top the trees with plums, she's freer than an eye, bird uncovered
in her gut, when he found her unevenly nailed, christ child
among barroom vagabonds, oh mistaken one in the center,
oh ready hoof—

I find then the law that
could only offer a perverse negation
fainting spells...resentment...
for in my inner being
a delight in the law
dipping his pen into the inkwell
not all of me joins in that delight

touching the pages
our creation is that teacher
I see another law at work
and the duration of our life
stealing anguished glances
is that teacher
against the law of my mind
our trials and death is that teacher
wretched man that I am

finding was that the anthologies provide a succinct example not of Ashton's claims, but of something that could be seen as almost the reverse. The

Sybil

They came in the night & it was the food that they thought.
Spasms and telepathy of spine, the nerves in catechism,
It was not the numeric page of the universe humming me
to a river of the dead; not the charge
& discharge of fate, Sybil's cry to be nothing.
                      I am a nightmarist by trade.
It was food that they sought, or sometimes
Symbol, fixed, like if you walked up a hill by a burned tree
and sang it meant birth. I try to catalogue each one, where gathered,
where unraveling. When I wake up, the house is moving. A sea-
wall coming and I, nailed to a plank. Every day
the notebook's icicles gleam on my pillow case.
This one still echoes: *I kept trying to die and couldn't.*
Each time my veins briefly brimmed with the unto of the unto—

―――――――――――

there is always a teacher nearby
two feet on the fender
and there is the teacher beyond
who will rescue this body of death
at the doors
able to touch the economy
I offer all my efforts to that teacher

Guru Brahma
Guru Vishnu
Guru Devo Maheshvara
Guru Sak Shat
Param Bhrama
Das May Shri Guruve Namaha
Das May Shri Guruve Namaha

L=A=N=G=U=A=G=E* Book** published in 1984 had 19% women in it, while the ***Outlaw Bible published in 1999 had only 23% women. A very modest

I still believe art may function to challenge the state, and not act in the service of it.

It is a choice.

To liberate art, over and over again.

To speak a body untethered from the so-called aims of narrative and economy.

Points of Pressure
Caroline Bergvall

I first gave this talk, in LA in April 2007[1], in the context of a culture that publicly exacerbates and condones actions of pointing, of naming, of showing the finger, of giving face. It has been happening to us, around us, slowly within us. Actions of pointing, of naming, of denouncing. That claim the enemy in our midst, not the enemy within. Don't let this be my finger. We have moved from the greedy liberalism of "don't ask don't tell" to the authoritarian religiosity of the one and only. From official silence to official silencing, or indeed its upshot, collective hysteria. "The war on terror inevitably reduces active dissent."[2] Both in Britain, where I live most of the time, and in America where I frequently share my work, political and juridical agendas such as the nature of citizenship, national identity and national language as well as cultural protectionism are squarely on the agenda. As a participant in a transnational poetics culture, my personal sense of what might constitute "us" and "we" is distended and contextual, finds its

improvement. Overall, in our admittedly arbitrary counting of mixed gender anthologies, we found that while women have been editing and publishing single

The Laughing Medusa
Meiling Cheng

"I shall speak about women's writing: about *what it will do*."[1] Thus began Cixous in her by now classic manifesto for *l'écriture féminine*, which is often cited in Anglo-American feminist criticism as "feminine writing," "female-sexed texts," or "a writing said to be feminine." More recently, Cixous referred to *écriture féminine* as a "decipherable libidinal femininity which can be read in writing produced by a male or a female,"[2] emphasizing the concept as a transgender writerly quality independent from its author's given sexual identity. Cixous's anti-essentialist fine-tuning of her concept does not bring us closer to the secret of deciphering "femininity" in writing. Nevertheless, as she argues, the fact that it's impossible to define or theorize a feminine writing practice doesn't mean that it doesn't exist.[3] If we suspend our judgment for a moment, we may approach "The Laugh of the Medusa" as an embodiment of this practice, inscribing the drive of a libidinal economy that can be perceived as "feminine" but cannot

---

allegiance across all sorts of borders. I'm a visitor, sometimes a resident, rarely a full citizen where I live. In a way, this is all part of the equation. Indeed, it is in light of this mood that I understand what seems like a resurgence or perhaps just a jolt of interest in feminism and feminist art, its commitment to social and political change. I want to know if and how we would run with it as writers and artists today.

•

The large art shows that have been up this past year in the US, such as the WACK show at MOCA, the one in Brooklyn, *High Times, Hard Times* at the National Academy Museum in NY, the consecration of Judy Chicago's *Dinner Party* as a permanent exhibit, but also the recent female poetry conference in Britain, feminist issues in art magazines, or international celebrations around Beauvoir's *Second Sex* all indicate a commemorative and historialising mood in regards to feminism's short history. Yet the art shows were so big, so packed with works, mostly from the late '50s to late '70s, that the impression has ended up being not so much on the work or their aesthetics as on a generation of politically

**gender volumes since the 1970s, they remain underrepresented in experimental/
postmodern/avant-garde/innovative mixed gender anthologies both before and**

be decoded. "The Laugh of the Medusa" does not so much speak "about" women's writing as enact, through its textual materiality, a particular woman's writing practice. The piece performs Cixous's own "femininity," her authorial subjectivity, rather than states programmatically the wherewithal of all writings by women-identified authors.

•

Cixous's italicized stress on feminine writing as that which not only states but also does something recalls J. L. Austin's distinction between constative and performative utterances. Austin defines a performative statement as one that cannot be considered "true or false," that does not "describe" or "report" or "constate" anything, and that its very utterance constitutes the "doing of an action" rather than merely "saying something."[4] In this light, "The Laugh of the Medusa" emerges as a piece of performative writing, a product of Cixous's writerly action that self-reflexively reveals the process of being made as simultaneously both the means and the end of her art. A paper performance whose textual boundary delimits its performative agency and site of action, it displays the navigation of an active will to writing within a specific spacio-temporal nexus, delineating

---

motivated female artists and social activists. It is ironic that the sheer wealth of work on display in each of these shows make us less likely to examine them in light of art history than in light of social participation and the political mood of the time. The shows seem to document these artworks primarily as the result of forms of critical gathering.

And yet the works on display are formally amazingly diverse and ambitious, a clear indication of the urgent engagement with aesthetic experimentation, as much as with social protest through it. They are a reminder of an optimism towards the validity of art as an aspect of collective action, and of the transformative power of individual risk and of critical imagination that is sorely and painfully lacking today, when again we need it most. The public mood is nervous, its taste and values increasingly conservative. Most of our celebrated artists are busy with commerce and success. In Britain, for instance, the YBAs have come of age and all we hear talk of relates to their personal branding and greed. A strange numbness, political disenfranchisement, the need for personal comfort, paired with professional achievement and isolation into art specialisms have all become powerful factors in preventing the vitality of collective identification. As has the

after the mid-'80s, both before and after *Moving Borders*. // But of course the anthologies only tell part of a complicated story. We wondered if it was just that

how Cixous intersected with "the Parisian publishing scene in the 1970s."⁵ It documents the breath, pulse, tremors, and obsessions of a particular historical and personal moment in women's liberation movement.

•

Above all, Cixous treats writing as a body-based action. "The Laugh of the Medusa" endorses the analogies between a writer and a performer, a reader and a spectator, for the essay is both a text and a meta-text infused with theatricality. The theatrical paradigm is discernible in Cixous's frequent direct addresses to her reader through the pronoun "you" and in her attempt to write in the present, basking in the pleasure of what she calls "theatrical time"—the "instant—the eternity of the instant," or "the rapidly pervasive now."⁶ Along with the performative dyad of writer and reader, a minimum of two actions is implicated: the original live action through which Cixous composed the text and the subsequent action that unfolds with the present-tense exchange between the text and its reader. The original action was private and inaccessible to the reading public, whereas the subsequent action can replenish itself ceaselessly so long as there is a reader for this text. "The Laugh of the Medusa" therefore brings

---

devaluation of imagination's anarchism. Formally, there's a standardisation of the progressive gestures inherited from the early avant-gardes as much as from the art and identity revolutions of the '60s and '70s, now absorbed into art techniques; a saturation for instance, of formal applications of appropriative and disjunctive techniques, art applying itself to its own tried methods, rather than looking for new ways of challenging the status quo and formal history. Ideally, one would hope that rather than being a historicisation of female artists' forms of protest, these shows would provoke in us our own renewed attention as gendered artists/critics/beings to forms of art and dissent that favour collective voicing and new realms of imaginings.

Seen in this light, the impulse behind these giant art-shows would seem less generational and more productive. As when Hélène Cixous wrote that: "In our impassioned times on all political fronts, where it is largely a question of an open and covert struggle with the mysteries of sexual difference, as women we are at the *obligatory* [her emphasis] mercy of simplifications"³. The fact that Cixous is pointing to, and perhaps warning about, the crudeness with which embodied politics are still at work in society is a reminder, if ever we needed

anthologies, which tend to have an already happened sort of staleness to their collecting, were out of whack, or if other parts of the experimental/postmodern/

into relief a succession of bodies surrounding a textual performance: from the laboring body of Cixous, who both came before and coincided with the body of her text, to those other bodies who came after, receiving her text. While Cixous's body of 1975 no longer exists as it did by the time she completed the writing, her writing's textual body remains conceptually renewable, as it begins to form itself again in 2007 with my process of reading it and, again, with your process of heeding my writing about it.

•

"And why don't you write? Write! Writing is for you, you are for you; your body is yours, take it," urges Cixous, submitting her writing as a coaxing for other women to write. Cixous has declared bluntly, "I am not a feminist"[7]; yet, her proactive feminine writing does seek an affective alliance with other women for she identifies herself as "a woman," writing "toward women." (78) Selecting writing as her medium, Cixous commits herself to two goals: "to break up, to destroy; and to foresee the unforeseeable, to project." (78) For Cixous, what must be destroyed but the "parental-conjugal phallocentrism" (79) that has hitherto reduced women to silence?

---

one, that things are far from how one might have hoped they would be. And that identification might again be inevitable as strategy. She continues: "In order to defend women we are obliged to speak in the feminist terms of 'man' and 'woman'." Given the virulence with which Cixous has spent most of her writing career denying the value of the feminist denomination, and feminist collectivity around the gendered assignation of woman or of women, starting from when it was most in view, in the '70s and just after May '68, does this extraordinary statement show a change of tactics?

•

The specific fighting that was feminism in the '70s and the scandal it has always caused, and still causes, is about oppositionality and collectivity, and it is representational in nature. It stems from the idea that it must be possible to speak and act across the cultural interdictions set up by gender hierarchy. As a parallel to this, the controversial British social thinker Paul Gilroy looks to the political and intellectual energy of earlier women's movements, and sees in their radical rethinking of gender and its social ramifications an important historical step that

avant-garde/innovative scene reflected similar gender troubles. // We briefly looked more in-depth at Silliman's blog. This was because our thinking and

And what can be foreseen if not the projection of female subjectivity unto the archival scrim of human history? As Cixous argues, "writing is precisely *the very possibility of change*, the space that can serve as a springboard for subversive thought, the precursory movement of a transformation of social and cultural structures" (81). If subversion is her motivation, then transformation is her goal.

•

Cixous's revisionary feminist project crystallizes in the image of the Medusa envisioned in her title. Here Medusa is laughing, invitingly, with a sensuous abandon rather than transfixing the invaders with a petrifying gaze: "You only have to look at the Medusa straight on to see her. And she's not deadly. She's beautiful and she's laughing" (85). Reclaiming an abject female archetype from the patriarchal Greek myths, Cixous converts the Gorgon's fabled monstrosity to be an exuberant show of vitality. Her iconoclastic positioning renders Medusa into a feminine/feminist talisman at the entrance to her eponymous text.

According to Alicia Le Van, Medusa was originally an aspect of the Great Triple Goddess in Africa, worshipped as the Serpent-Goddess of the Libyan Amazons. Prior to her absorption into the Athenian mythology, Medusa

---

is also conducive in trying to effect the necessary process of "the denaturation of race" that he advocates in his work. The many disputes of feminism are a question of boundaries and of terrain rather than of strict genealogy. It is useless to trace up smooth continuities and lineages when the mapping of engagement runs across so many divergent methodological and conceptual lines, as well as cultural histories. One must just take what one needs to work and think. Poets such as Adrienne Rich, Nicole Brossard, June Jordan, were crucial activists, brilliant theorists and polemicists of their generation, political poets, and for their purposes, they had divergent ideas about woman, but agreed on the fact that as cultural axis, "she" is a symbol of necessary revolution, a complicated dare, that must be contextualised in relation to class, ethnicity, cultural belonging. Feminism has been a collective yet conflicted password; women, a heterogeneous potential; and Freud's dark continent, "a rose wet cave." These things were difficult to say, didn't sit easily in language, nor in culture and one needed to carve inroads. These things are still difficult to say, and still easily derided.

questioning began there. Also Silliman's inclusive and expansive and leftist personality led us to think that he might be someone who would be susceptible

was associated with the procreative, destructive, and regenerative power of "sovereign female wisdom," with visual representations featuring labyrinth, vaginal, uterine, and other central core designs.[8] Medusa's status as an African transplant to Europe recalls the similar trajectory taken by Cixous, who was born in the French colony of Algeria to a Spanish/French/Jewish father and German/Jewish mother and who later moved to Europe when the Algerian war broke out in 1956. Medusa's awesome otherness to the Olympian pantheon of Gods might have reminded Cixous of her own frequently-professed triple marginalization—"as a woman, as a Jew, as an Algerian colonial."[9] By analogy, I see Medusa as an alter ego for Cixous—or, to borrow from Cixous's expression elsewhere: "The one is the double or the metaphor of the other."[10] "The Laugh of the Medusa" is, in this autobiographical context, a performance of Cixous's "self" via the guise of a recuperated mythic character. The author is the actor who embodies the dramatic persona, who in turn emerges as a stand-in for the actor's self. A woman must "write her self," urges Cixous's text. "By writing her self, woman will return to the body which has been more than confiscated from

•

As a poetic and semiotic investigation of subjectivity, of identity, of difference, the notion of the feminine was in the '70s very differently both a tool for fighting-as-lucid-dreaming and a methodological tool for unpacking hierarchical blindspots lodged in and revealed by discourse. It advocated first and foremost the development of sophisticated individualised practices informed by ideas of sexual difference. It was and is explicitly a discursive practice, rooted in semiotic disturbance. Its revolt is psychic and philosophical. It deploys eroticised, pulsing, energetic "feminised" body imagery to challenge and subvert the very idea of identity. It did and continues to lead to fundamentally exploratory views of writing, and of the gendered subject, based on practices of reading, and the reassessing and unpacking of existing texts. Aspects of this can be found, in related ways, in the critical carnival of body-related performances, postcolonial works, queer arts and diverse other practices. In the '70s, the feminine "streaks through official texts, illuminating subtexts and subliminal noises as letters swerve, collide, coagulate in the wound-the scar in scarlet-the

in the best sense of the term to "feminist interventions." We counted what we thought of as single author posts (and we admit that we had to be interpretative

---

her" (81). "The Laugh of the Medusa" offers Cixous precisely an opportunity to write herself, to complete an auto-inscription enabled by the name of Medusa.

How do these two interwoven entities—the writer's body and her self—relate to the title character, Medusa? Cixous's body is a corporeal site in which her self dwells, from which she never departs, but through which she travels to the world of others. By writing her self she seizes her embodied existence as a liberating condition that affords her the agency to determine and execute her course of action. As readers, we do not encounter this body in the flesh, but rather, in the flesh made of the writer's words, a linguistic corpus that evokes the writer's self whenever the pronoun "I" appears. "I," the name with which an authorial subject voices her self, has no desire to stand alone. As an initiator in a verbal exchange, the "I" always anticipates the presence of a "you," the other body that views and verifies the exchange. To put it in Cixous's phrasing, "No I without you ever or more precisely no I's without you's. I is always our like."[11]

In "The Laugh of the Medusa," "our like" is either another woman or a collective of women; "our like" is Cixous's intended readership as she announces at the outset and reiterates throughout.

---

scars of historical/etymological silences" writes Joan Retallack suggestively.[4] To assert through negative affirmation, as French feminists and post-structuralists including Cixous did, that no-one has any idea what a woman is, and where the boundaries between inner and outer go, highlighted the pervasive scandal and disciplining that gender represents at the heart of social practice, embodiment and language

•

In an interview with his American translator Carl Weber, the German playwright Heiner Müller receives the following question: "In many of your texts you deal with topics which in this country would be defined as 'feminist'; and female characters often have a central place in your work. Could you explain how you think women should be presented on the contemporary stage?" Müller replies: "As a playwright I don't deal with 'isms' but with reality. Can you tell me what a real female character is?"[5] Elsewhere he questions not only how to trace up the specific reality of a female character but more broadly, and this is how it also hangs together for me, the validity of the theatrical stage itself to continue to

about what was and was not a "single author post"), and we found that there were around 127 about men and around 42 that were about women, or that

So, let me ask again, who is Medusa? She is a mythic female archetype who fends off aggression by interacting with others through her sight and whose body melds together multiple creatures across the species lines, including woman (her face), snake (her hair), bird (her wings), and fish (her scaly neck). The triad of femininity, interactivity, and multiplicity finds a dynamic embodiment in Medusa's image. The Gorgon's mythic body provides various cues regarding how Cixous structures and substantiates her textual body. The woman in Medusa engenders Cixous's text as feminine; her wings allow the text to fly, meeting Cixous's claim that "Flying is woman's gesture" (87); the scales in her neck make the text slippery, hence easier to evade surveillance and codification. Most remarkable among these is the writhing torsos of those living snakes that crown, contour, and empower Medusa's head, which is morphologically multiplied into many heads, many beginnings. This cranial convergence of many heads transmutes into the Cixousian style of beginning again and again, as she strives to do away with the logic of sequential argument. Like the multiple snakeheads that keep Medusa acutely aware of her environment, Cixous's ever-incipient paragraphs are the perceptual sensors that support the liquid luminescence of her textual body.

---

affect processes of confrontation and awareness. He readily envisages a future culture where the theatre's function, and therefore art and culture as it exists today, will have been completely transformed by changed social needs. In what kind of a culture will gender have been completely transformed?

•

Gertrude Stein said that prepositions are "the thing that can of all things be most mistaken."[6] Let's suggest that woman is preposition. What does *of, by, with, into, under, towards* reveal? What kind of directionality and discursive operations externalise, denaturalise identity into its gestures, its performance, its likelihood, so that everything starts to highlight the structure where there used to be Nature, or the syntactical rule of gendering where there used to be something real? For some, like the British poet and feminist theorist Denise Riley, it is good to know that "I am a woman only sometimes."[7] So timed a woman. Sometimes I man a wooing. All wool to some eyes. "I don't know myself," writes Cixous. She continues: "We could think over these mysteries [mysteries of gender and gender identification] but we don't. We are unable to inscribe or write them

women made up about 25% of these posts, during the first year that Silliman began the blog (from December 2002 to November 2003). // In the years that

As Cixous states in "Coming to Writing": "In the beginning, there is an end. Don't be afraid: it's your death that is dying. Then: all the beginnings. When you have come to the end, only then can Beginning come to you."¹² Theoretically, any writer may experience the void that feels like an end in the beginning of writing. When the writer is a woman, however, the void that greets her verbal action acquires additional gravity, for she cannot but write in a language steeped in phallogocentrism, which has historically spelt her out as the abyss, the lack, the second sex. Thus, when a woman writes, she begins willfully ending her suppression by inserting her presence, her subjectivity, into the archives of letters. The dying that she survives is, then, the death of her silence in a language that has for a long time excluded her. In her Genesis, the world does not begin with a male-gendered word, but with the possibilities of many more beginnings: she creates, and she procreates.

---

since we don't know who we are, something we never consider since we always take ourselves for ourselves; and from this point on we no longer know anything. I'll tell you frankly that I haven't the faintest idea who I am, but at least I know I don't know."⁸ For Judith Butler, to give an account of oneself retains a degree of opacity. It isn't so much about professed ignorance, this could prove self-congratulatory, as about partial view. This notion of opacity is about non-transmission, local untranslatability. This body is both already translated (by gender, say) (by daily commute, say) (by having an accent, say) and remains also in part non-translatable, non-reducible along representational lines.⁹ This makes my address necessarily contextual and could guarantee an effort towards difference. Butler calls it responsibility. To be different to one's perceived self. To envisage that the other is different from what I envisage them to be. To begin to see everything and everybody from this angle. "We are not mere dyads on our own, since our exchange is conditioned and mediated by language, by conventions, by a sedimentation of norms that are social in character and that exceed the perspective of those involved in the exchange."¹⁰ Not I love you, but I love TO you. Now here's a great use of a preposition. "I love TO

followed, several fairly intense "feminist interventions" happened. One was from Silliman himself who noted in 2002 that he gets attacked in his comment

Works Cited:

1. Hélène Cixous. "The Laugh of the Medusa," trans. Keith Cohen and Paula Cohen. *The Women and Language Debate: A Sourcebook*, ed. Camille Roman, Suzanne Juhasz, Cristanne Miller. New Brunswick, NJ: Rutgers University Press, 1994. 78-93. This version, originally published in Signs (Summer 1976), is a revised version of "Le rire de la méduse," which appeared in L'arc 61 (1975): 39-54. All citations of Cixous's text come from this source.
2. Verena Andermatt Conley. *Hélène Cixous: Writing the Feminine*. Lincoln and London: University of Nebraska Press, 1984. 129. The book includes the appendix "An Exchange with Hélène Cixous," 129-161.
3. I paraphrase Cixous's original passage, which goes as follows: "It is impossible to define a feminine practice of writing, and this is an impossibility that will remain, for this practice can never be theorized, enclosed, coded—which doesn't mean that it doesn't exist," in "The Laugh of the Medusa." 84.
4. J. L. Austin. *How to Do Things with Words*, ed. J. O. Urmson and Marina Sbisà, Second Edition. Cambridge: Harvard University Press, 1997 [1962].
5. See Gayatri Chakravorty Spivak. "Cixous Without Borders." *On the Feminine*, ed. Mireille Calle, trans. Catherine McGann. New Jersey: Humanities Press, 1996. 50.
6. Hélène Cixous. "In October 1991 . . .." *On the Feminine*, 77. The second citation comes from "The Laugh of the Medusa." 84.
7. Toril Moi. *Sexual/Textual Politics: Feminist Literary Theory*. London: Routledge, 1985. 103.

---

you," writes Luce Irigaray. The phrase is grammatically awkward. It proposes a dynamic directionality, not fusion, nor emotive immersion, but a conscious separateness yet connection in the form taken by the lovers and their address to each other, and by extension their tentative availability to the world. Love is direction, positioning. It is the apprenticeship of reciprocity. A poetic traffic based on the complexities of exchange and of separateness. It tries to bridge current difficulties in establishing communal yet differential dialogue. It makes it explicitly mysterious, not self-evident to know how to talk about oneself as a gendered being. And how to talk to someone else.

For a long time, I've been working out of pressure points, awkward grammatical and cultural units that force up questions about linguistic belonging, bodyshape, the communal bonds or binds or bounds that lodge within my own make-up. I know for instance that I appear as a non-native English speaker. I also appear as female and white. Do I declare myself so, and how or why would I do this? Is this a framing I can avoid? A framing I need? A framing you need? How do I declare myself or appear to function? How many terms are necessary or viable? Is it as necessary for one's poetics as it is for one's

box almost every time he posts on a woman while when he writes on men, he gets attacked about one time out of ten. Another was the particularly venomous

8. Alicia Le Van, "The Gorgon Medusa," *Women in Antiquity*, 7 May 1996. http://www.perseus.tufts.edu/classes/finALp.html.
9. See Lynn Kettler Penrod, *Hélène Cixous*. New York: Twayne Publishers, 1996. 1.
10. Hélène Cixous, "Preface," *The Hélène Cixous Reader*, ed. Susan Sellers. London: Routledge, 1994. xv. In the original context, the cited passage is Cixous's description of her inseparability from the world.
11. Ibid, xvii.
12. From Cixous, "Coming to Writing," cited by Penrod in *Hélène Cixous*, New York: Twayne Publishers, 1996. 1.

---

civic life? Surely they don't all apply at once nor all the time. But how do I appear to speak as a female, trilingual, queer, White European, EU resident in London? How do I announce points of obvious or difficult visibility not primarily as points of belonging, but rather as moments of contact and of contract with the world? That said, does that make me anything else? From now on make me nothing else? That's it sorted. Sweat under the collar because boxes tick me off. Ticking not only confirms but forces outwardness. The arrow says that way. Now point that finger. Mostly it feels like walking into a glass-door or cube. Like measuring one's sleeping quarters. Yet declared as much by what I'm not. Or by what I remain unaware of being. An Amharic speaking sax-player in the clubs of Addis Abbabba. A Spanish film-maker in the streets of Paris. Large birds in vast blue cedar trees. And Kafka was a dog. And Clarice Lispector became a cockroach. This is everything to me. Metonymic, interdependent stretch and animal extensions live in the grass skin of one's humanness, throw open a call to the unknown and the obscure, as much as to the around. Truth then, not in what I say I am, but in all I am with. In all I accept to be with? In all I accept to be?

•

response by several commentators to a positive post that Silliman wrote about Barbara Jane Reyes in March 2006. And then there was the October 2006

Daguerreotype of a Girl
Lidia Yuknavitch

Menas 1

You must picture your image of Eastern Europe.
In your mind's eye.
Whatever that image is.
However it came to you.
Winter.

One winter night when she is not a child (was she ever a child?), Menas walks outside, her shoes against snow, her arms cradling a self, her back to a house not her house but housing her. It is a night after the blast that has atomized her family and any sense of an identity. Some years.

But that night has never left her... unrelenting bruise. It's blue-black image pearling in and out of memory.

In the long run, the most radical domino effect of questioning identity must be that it is felt through the entire tissue. Social, mental, perceptual. Paul Gilroy has called this the necessity to "learn to practice a systematic form of disloyalty to our own local civilisation if we seek to understand or interact equitably with others formed elsewhere."[11] Foreigners have the animal in them. Cixous's perception of writing as an exploration of embodied language emerges from cultural displacement. In a sense, her view of language and writing stems not only from being occupied by gender, but also from her colonised background as an Algerian Jew of European descent, brought up speaking German in a French and Arabic context. For many bicultural artists and writers, the processes of identity and of writing acquisition go hand in hand with aspects of cultural belonging and the way this articulates their lived body and speaking voice. When the writer's cultural and social body accommodates two or three languages and/or cultures, their inscriptive narratives and poetics are necessarily at a break from a monolingual textual body-type and a nationally defined writing culture. It is often accompanied by a propensity towards open-forms and mixed genres, remains dubious and questioning of defining terms, can be resistant of exile or

complaint by Elizabeth Treadwell on her blog about a blurb Silliman had written of Patti McCarthy's book *Verso*. The blurb that was eventually published

Nor will it ever leave her body, the blast forever injuring her spine, so that all of her life she will carry pain like the story of histories unspoken, and since she will grow into a woman with intelligence and intuition and artistic integrity, she will almost never speak of it. She will transform unbearable pain into artistic production—exactly like how women take what turns out to be a life and live with it.

Nations move over the small backs of children, grinding their bones and hearts into the earth.

The white of the snow stretches out like the bones of a human hand.

You know, we act as if children are always under development, and thus unable to mourn or register the fact of an identity, having not quite arrived. It is not true. It may be more true that identity is as fully formed as the cosmos, as DNA, as geographic actuality in the first moments of life. The open mouth as gaping as a galaxy. The unconscious wail. The physical violence. The irrelevancy of time or space.

The moon's giant white eye.

The moon pulls her eyes, bathes her lightly, convinces her night is not any kind of ending, but rather the place of dreams and visions and beginnings. She

---

immigrant narratives and their inward longing for a traditionalist past where identities are firmly locked in place, rather than in play.[12]

•

Feminism acted as the launch pad for multiple and ongoing critical collectivities. Whether admitted to or not, it did change our perception of the world. For this reason, in the great scheme of things, it matters little today whether one's individual impulse towards feminism is weary of collective identification or not, is anti-feminist, feminist or feminoid, whether content comes to form or form comes to content. What I think might matter more is how to act in the knowledge of these many fronts and sometimes antagonistic yet co-existent phases of cultural and social history. Fronts through which Western culture experienced a denaturation, yet not neutralisation, of its big essentialist narrative categories, of which gender, race, sexuality, history. What I think might matter more is how to keep on making art from contingent and insurrectional terrains. How to step out of isolation and find ways of making a meal out of one's art, and out of one's bones. It is difficult to stay precise, close to one's chest, aware of how to use

on the book goes like this: "Pattie McCarthy has been one of our most intellectually ambitious poets—a tradition she shares with Rachel Blau DuPlessis

is older than a child who would chase the moon, so when she decides to follow it, it is with the sure-footedness of the in-between girlhood of things.

The moon.

Like the iris of an eye, a circle within a circle. She moves forward deeper into the dark and open, away from the house not hers.

The snow becomes apparent now, and she wishes she had a coat. She wishes she had tied her shoes properly, worn socks. The moon, however, makes an entire setting for her motion, and in this way she feels…lit up.

She thinks of the moment of the blast, the singular fire lighting up the face of her father, her mother, first yellow, then orange and blue, then white, then nothing. Of course this is and isn't true. The moment was a flash of white, a sound closing hearing. It is only in memory that she has changed the pacing to slow motion, changed the colors to vivid hues electrifying her mind.

This does not frighten her. What used to be nightmares have transformed into color and light, composition and story, song and tune. It is with her now. Lifelong companion. Still life of a dead family.

---

privilege, prejudice, one's positioning in the world, all the while trying to throw a line into the pot. Good to know how to use what one identifies with, this shifts the shadows about. For this reason, located and gendered identity is crucial, however faulty and open-ended. Sort of clarifies that there is problem. Forbids any easy equation, but makes the terms available to be worked on and worked out. It is also good to realise how one is used by what one identifies with.

The value of dislocation, of being disorientated, which in itself calls on more movement, is part of the process of orientation. What escapes the known of the settled escapes the possible of the lodged, escapes the very idea of being "here" once one accepts that one is lost, that one is getting lost, becoming lost, staying lost while looking for new directions. We open up our own narratives, those we think we know, and register that we don't know where they go from here. Again, we start with that. Jane Blocker in her excellent study on the exile Cuban artist Ana Mendieta, writes that "understanding identity as having these 'performative' qualities enables a discussion of gender, color, nation, and ethnicity that […] allows us to ask "<u>where</u> is Ana Mendieta (implying contingency), instead of, "<u>who</u> is Ana Mendieta? (implying an unconditional truth)."[13] What still matters is

& with H.D. And indeed with the likes of Pound & Olson. We can still count the number of women who attempt writing on such a scale on the fingers of our

    She keeps following, or is she leading? She moves in the dark over the snow under the moon. She thinks of folktales and gypsies. Horses. She sees the moon's light and suddenly night turns to be something else. She sees a white field ahead of her—a great white field—stretched out like paper or canvas. She stops and her breath fogs in front of her, sweet articulation of wonder. Of desire. She is in love with the white spread before her.

    Its purity and readiness.

    Its virginity. Like that of a girl.

    A girl not her.

    A girl not ravaged.

    Its potential—like a waiting body.

    Then she hears something not her and not the night and not the white expanse waiting before her. Her feet are cold and she can suddenly feel how numb her hands are shoved in her armpits. She does not know what she hears at first. At first it seems as if it is the sound of hummingbirds' wings, but that is not possible. A fluttering whir, quiet as secrets, there and then gone.

    Then she does know what she hears.

---

not first and foremost where you're from, or what you're from, it's where you're at, it's how you act and move along the sets of points and pointers that make you.

Works Cited

1. This version is a substantial, yet not structural, rewrite of the talk delivered at Feminaissance.
2. Gilroy, Paul. *Postcolonial Melancholia*. New York: Columbia University Press, 2005. 73.
3. Cixous, Hélène. *Three Steps on the Ladder of Writing*. New York: Columbia University Press, 1993. 52.
4. Retallack, Joan. *The Poethical Wager*. Berkeley: University of California Press, 2003. 106.
5. Müller, Heiner. *Hamletmachine and Other Texts for the Stage*. Ed. Carl Weber. vols. New York: Performing Arts Journal Publications, 1984. 139.
6. Stein, Gertrude. "Poetry and Grammar." *Look at Me Now and Here I Am: Writings and Lectures, 1909-45*. Ed. Patricia Meyerowitz. Harmondsworth: Penguin, 1971. 127.
7. Riley, Denise. *Am I That Name?: Feminism and the Category of 'Women' in History*. Basingstoke: Macmillan, 1988.
8. Sellers, Susan, ed. *The Hélène Cixous Reader*. New York London: Routledge, 1994. 200.
9. Butler, Judith. *Giving an Account of Oneself*. New York: Fordham University Press, 2005. 39.
10. Ibid. 28.
11. Gilroy, Paul. *Postcolonial Melancholia*. New York: Columbia University Press, 2005. 71

**hands. So it is worth noting & celebrating this addition to that roster."
Treadwell's response is a rousing call to all to notice the women writers around**

She hears something so familiar it is foreign to her. She hears a wolf caught in a trap. She looks down near a fence line she barely noticed was there…ha. Like the divisions between nations. There one minute, gone the next, loyalties and allies disintegrated into snow or rain or DNA. What a trick history, geography, being is.

She looks to the left—it is what she thought. It is a beautiful beyond beautiful wolf with its leg caught in a trap. She moves closer, now aware that she is freezing to death (a phrase "freezing to death" which is a bit comical in eastern Europe). The wolf is smart. It is almost finished. She thinks of releasing it only in the briefest of thoughts and then abandons the thought.

The wolf is nearly free.

In its freedom it will lose a leg.

It will be worth it.

The freedom will be won.

She holds perfectly still.

More still than a dead person.

Which she has seen, many times, a corpse in snow.

---

12. I have discussed this elsewhere in relation to the work of Theresa Hak Kyung Cha's *Dictee*, Lisa Linn Kanae's volume *Sista Tongue*, Rosmarie Waldrop's *Key to the Language of America*, and Erin Moure's complex translative poetic practice.

13. Jane Blocker. *Where Is Ana Mendieta?: Identity, Performativity, and Exile*. Durham: Duke University Press. 25.

them and how their numbers exceed ten." // Then we recounted the single author posts for the year 2006 and what we found was that there were 61 on men

Still life against white. Against all of humanity.

It takes nearly an hour, but the wolf finally frees herself.

She is suddenly sure it is a female. Females carry the endurance of all of humanity. The long wait waiting. The bearing of life. The bearing of death. The wolf frees itself in a single glorious excruciating moment—it lets out a cry larger than an infant's.

It is then that she does something, well, thoughtless. Something so intuitive it could only be the mark of an artist. She goes to where the rust-orange and black metal of the trap sits holding its severed limb, she goes to where blood and animal labor have reddened and dirtied the pristine white of the snow—like the violence against a page or canvas—without thinking, she pulls down her pants, her underwear, she squats with primal force and pisses and pisses there where the crime happened.

Her eyes close.

Her mouth fills with spit.

It is, or more accurately, it will become, the most erotic moment of her life.

The First Gurgitation is a Sentence
Vanessa Place & Carolyn K. Place (H. Jan 6, 2007)

Is she here?
No.
She didn't come?
No.
She didn't come?
She couldn't make it.
But I did this all for her!
I know.
(La règle du jeu)

Is she here?   The first gurgitation is a sentence. No.   *I*
She didn't come?   *am the picture of health...just ask anyone.*
No.   The sentence is a container of
She didn't come?   thought, *(La règle du jeu)*

75

and 27 on women, or that women now made up 31% of these. In other words, once again our instincts were wrong; the feminist interventions were not

>   She will develop a need to piss when she comes.
>   It will drive away men.
>   Women.
>   It will attract men.
>   Women.
>   This is how our sexuality is formed—a frame at a time—against white, taboo, thoughtless, corporeal. Our psyches writing themselves against our very beings.
>   A wolf running three-legged against white into the savior of blackness, from which all creativity springs.
>   A girl healing herself even as healing appears impossible. Healing herself through sexual release. Through artistic production. Through the endless act of making.
>   She opens her eyes.
>   The piss smell and the blood smell and the youth smell of her skin mingle.
>   Salt of all being.
>   She licks her lips.

---

                              compositional,
                                    rolling as a
She couldn't make it.   shopping
But I did this all for her!   cart.
I know.   (La règle du jeu)
(La règle du jeu)   The point   No.
              Is she here? She didn't come? I did this all for
her!
El lenguaje como fenomeno estetico
              I know.   (La règle du jeu) She couldn't make it.
       being
          the following: Is she here? Is she here?
                         No.
                         She didn't come?
    No.   No.   No.
                    She didn't come?

changing much. Even during the year in which they happened. After our original thought that the "feminist interventions" were actively changing the

She places her hands into the blood and reprints them in a clean, white place.

What is a girl but this—this obscene and beautiful making against the expanse of white—this brilliant imagination inventing meaning.

And then she runs toward a self.

What is a girl?

Think Dr. Ellis got a bit put out with me for moaning about how relatively well I feel...a perverse view, I realize, but I just would like to know what will happen and when?? I know.
                                                            No.
                    Prepositions are relational.
     (La règle du jeu)
                                 She didn't come?
Is she here?   No.   Is she here?
He suggested I might want to think about some counseling, but wasn't too in favor of support groups.
No.
     She didn't come?   *(La*
        I know.   *règle*
        I know.   *du*
     She didn't come?   *jeu)*

representational politics of poetry tanked, we decided to look at some other categories. Despite a thriving small press scene, women still tend to be

> To you, we move about in the regular ways. But I tell you, we know each other. We look each other in the eye without speaking. We eat. We dance. We fuck. We mother. We write. We make our meanings. We take our chances.

Relations cathedral conjunctions. Conjunctions
        shiver the soft meat
            above
   the elbow. Fee simple, and
                complex, there is a glistening slit
            in
     the side of my sentence
           from
which I feed the forthcoming. They are watery-
               eyed, and
      have the fresh throats
         of
    toilets. They come
           on
their knees, but there's no pleasing me. I issue regular as a magazine, witness like chalk, and church mice. If I were an oyster, I'd be content with vinegar. If I were confined to a correctional facility, I'd compass your estate.

underrepresented. // • Roof Books, publishing since 1978, has published books by 43 men and 24 women (36% women). // • Subpress, publishing since 1999,

Figuring the Imaginary: Writing into the Strange Genitalia,
or Notes Towards a Fabular Irradiated Accelerate Social Imaginary
Bhanu Kapil

"Here's the book. Here's the book that I/ will not write. This is where it begins / Here is the book that I will never/ write, I thought." I love these words by Helene Cixous, I sometimes think, because they appear as abbreviated, translated notes in a reproduction of her *Writing Notebooks*. I'm also attracted to the fact that a text about writing is also a text about the "spectacular event" of her son's birth, who was born with Down's Syndrome, and also in the same breath, her coded notes on private sexual acts made public: "But only this. But who scratched you on the left cheek...what's happening/another different way of life/ It makes you jump—/I'm waiting for time to complete its rounds/ The subject of this letter" PLUS "The gent was a deadpan type. So—he said—you're going to be masturbating again." This is the interpolate imaginary I propose as the first body of this paper: a body capable of mating with itself, witnessing itself giving birth with "surprising results," and writing in a way that proposes the figure of the

---

Is she here?
No.

Anyway, the gist is I am coasting along...and doing nicely as most of the effects from the radiation are gone...He expressed some concern

(La règle du jeu) Is she here?

about   She didn't come.

(La règle du jeu) Is she here?

Organicism,   *(La règle du jeu)*
in little golden curls, with the brown-eyed changing sorrow of baby rats. Life neverlasting. Amen.

She couldn't make it.

No. No. She didn't come? She didn't come? She didn't come? No. No.

She couldn't make it.

79

has published books by 21 men, 9 women, and 1 person who identifies as transgender (or 32% women). // • Green Integer, publishing since 1997, has

writer writing: "only where I fail, I only write against…but it is something—it's a driving power whose law I try to obey."

•

I'm profoundly interested in the "driving power" of figuration, in how I might make, in books, female bodies (which are also immigrant bodies) that are both conjunctive and extensive (excess limbs proliferating from the torso; the tapetums of a wolfgirl's eyes adapting to nocturnal life, so that in a darkened room or in the jungle their eyes shine blue). Nevertheless, in thinking through the problem of how a female body is constructed, through the lens of mutation, it led me to the next question, the question of what such a body wants, really wants, which I asked my friends and neighbors (ranging from poets and theorists to the acupuncturist I share suite 105 of Sun Plaza with—I'm a massage therapist—and the Mary Kay agent who was visiting her office to give her a make-over): "If you were a monster," I asked them, "what kind of sex would you have?" These were some of their replies:

•

(La règle du jeu)
the 2nd site in the duodena as I do get upset stomach easily which isn't normal for me. I said that originally when the radiation people scanned that site, they couldn't tell if

That should be the end of it, but   I
we've calm reflection left. Time to   I
paddle in the river, piddle in the   I
bath. Breathing time, space to cogitate. We pray, and infinitives smack us in the middle face.
(La règle du jeu)
    (She couldn't make it.) (Is she here?)
               (No.)
                         know.
                         it was cancer
                       or merely an ulcer..

published 163 men and 45 women (or 22% women). // • Atelos, published 16 men and 11 women (or 41% women). // • Wave Books, has published 30 men

"Well, two monsters would vomit into each others' mouths and then they'd eat the sofa they were sitting on."

"Well, the leg, which would normally be retracted...the monster would have this mechanism to extend and then I would wrap around and she'd put her foot into his...you know."

"I'll think about it. I think writing into the strange genitalia is really necessary."

"Monster sex may not involve arms and torsos but it is heavily dependent upon whatever appendages they use to move (i.e. legs). Because if a monster is a critique of the status quo then it must be built for mobility (think of how even though zombies are slow-moving, they are unrelenting in their forward momentum). Monster sex: vomit, feeding, legs...and...I may have got it wrong in the sense that I don't exactly mean love, but internal heat."

"I picture big fluffy monsters going crazy on each other and then there's like a fluffy mass of fur and arms just flailing. (What color are monsters?) Blue. The blue from the monsters of *Monsters, Inc.*"

"I don't know. It's so intense. We used to take turns sitting on top of each other and take turns shitting. It was crazy."

She couldn't make it.   *(La règle du*

Ongoingness, beneath the artifice. I would be happy with a bowl of
cereal and some real cream. But I can't have without having
not. I've rolled my hair and pennies, taken in strays and strangers. "By" is
what I meant to say. The knives are kept in a chopping-block, and there's
a blue bottle marked "don't." Just as you willed me, and willed me to won't.
But
 now cats' paws have tattered the bigger books and
jeu) jeu) jeu) jeu) jeu) jeu) jeu)

and wondered if that could be the problem. He agreed it was possible so prescribed some OTC pills for ulcer patients (I suspect this is called

                                                                Is she here?

we've given up our first names, or insist on their exclusive use.
Everyone has his reason, That's what's terrible

                        (La règle du jeu)

and 17 women (or 36% women). // University presses are a little more complicated but a little more skewed to gender equity. // • Wesleyan, known for

Reading and listening to these descriptions of imagined and actual sex acts, I took great pleasure in the gross movements available to monsters, but also the unexpected, compulsive, almost subliminal properties of their desires: a mouthful of blue fur, or the body split open from the groin to the neck to become, temporarily, a unitary yet looping orifice then knit together, scarred over, to become a continuous membrane again. Why is continuity necessary? And does the insistence of a membrane reverse, in a regressive sense, the potentiality of rupture—does it, in fact, smooth it over? In thinking through the sexual construction of the monster, I kept coming back to the fact that we need a membrane because it contains the processes of life—of metabolism and variegated flows of all kinds—the lymph, the blood—and without it, as real bodies, we'd die. Even monsters, I discovered, fall in love, "want to make a go of it."

•

So, two notes here, towards how a fabular, irradiated, accelerate social imaginary—in the form of an extreme figure—how such a figure might be, could be, is—a force of "positive change":

———————

Autobiography, that's what counts.   But I did this all for her!
I care, I do. I care for me, and by
me, I'll care for you. This is the beauty of   No.
landed property, want sent silent and constant. This is the secret I'll take to
    She couldn't come.
the urinal. The crapper, I mean, where everyone's arraigned the
same. *(La règle du jeu)*
                                                     I know.
Three men are driving in the desert. Their car breaks down, and they each take
    one thing for the hike back to
town: the first man grabs a bottle of water, the second a sandwich, the
third the
car door. The first two men turn to their companion, and say: "If we get
thirsty, we have water. If we get hungry, a sandwich. But why the car door?"
The third man says, "If I get hot
                                         Is she here?
humoring the patient)..   *(La règle du jeu)*
                                         No.

publishing "mainly" women has 89 by men and 66 by women (or 43% women) // • The University of California, series has 10 books by men and 11 by women

1. Writing about what a body is and what a body might become also presents or opens up the deeper question of hybridity—not necessarily as a discourse interpolated with artistic content, but as a test. If you join a woman's body with a bird's body, then I want to know about how that impossible but felt or visible wing came into being. Was there blood loss? Were the wings sewn onto the body with aluminium thread, and if so, was the woman sedated during the procedure? Did it happen in a hospital, or did someone line the bed with plastic then set down some towels? What is the relationship of numbness to transgression? Where is the pain threshold and is the juncture between two kinds of flesh apparent to others? Can they see it, or is it concealed by a costume, by an expert hand, by the hand reaching out, like the hand in the preliminary stages of foreplay, to switch off the Pier One lamp on the rickety rattan table next to the bed? I want a cellular, attentive account. I want a kiss.

2. Though it's a given that such a body might possess peculiar and erratic freedoms, I want to know what it can't quite manage. For example, for a body, a hybrid construction, that's organized around a basic loss of control, the formidable absence—whether voluntarily or not—of social obligation, of

---

                                                 Does she breathe?
No.
No. *(La règle du jeu)*
                                    but I'll try

               (La règle du jeu) the window—it sticks. *(La règle du jeu)*
                    Now that I've glutted all the gods, and they
                              (La règle du jeu) bubble in
                              satisfaction, *(La règle du jeu)*
            She didn't come?   She couldn't make it.

      them for a couple of weeks to see if it helps. Anyway, when I came
                                                home I looked
        No.   there are fences   No.
                  and rabbits   No.
      up duodenal ulcer on the internet and believe the symptoms
  and still   She didn't come?
described

(or 52% women). // • **University of Iowa Press has 20 books by men; 20 books by women (or 50% women). // • The Pitt Poetry Series has done 70 books by**

conformity—I still want to know what's slipping through the fence. Or under it. I want to know what remains or simply is—uncontainable, unprocessed, and unmanageable. I suppose I want to know about an "unseen but recorded" experience of desire—not what we should desire or what fantastic, bad-good thing might happen—George Clooney, for example, sodomizing a female cyborg of Punjabi origin with his left foot— but desire in its vestigial state. What she feels. What she can't help feeling, though later, telling her friends, she says something else.

•

In trying to think through this idea of what is real for the social imaginary, and why it feels so essential to open up, in a weirdly conventional move, a more private or "imperceptible" space of feeling, I began an email exchange with my friend, Andrea Spain, a Deleuzean feminist scholar in Buffalo, New York. Me: "This might be a dumb question, but when Liz Grosz talks about the real, what does she mean?" Andrea: "You're not going to believe this…but the real is 'real', that which really happens. Or, I should say, the forces that are us and more than us produce the real. This production is what Deleuze calls desire."

———————————

(La règle du jeu)
I said I'd pray, there's no adverbial consolation.   By way of extension is
are very like what I am experiencing..aside from   I know.
what I meant to say.

                                          She couldn't make it.   No.
that he just

reiterated   No.

that   But I did it all for her!

there is no way to know   But I did it all for her!   No.

what will

happen or how

long…that

men and 64 by women (or 48% women). // Briefly leaving the experimental/ postmodern/avant-garde/innovative scene and looking at prizes, things get even

But what does this mean for experimental women's writing? I've tried, for this [book], to come up with strategies towards the future of the psycho-sexual document, a space in which the body could be overwhelmed by acts —pleasurable, blurry, intense and surprising—that, in turn, transform or distend the membrane—the physiological space a body inhabits. [...] To this end, I have begun to write about a state-sponsored "Haven" for chimps—former lab technicians, wracked with guilt, working as orderlies for peanuts, yet...was that Jimbo slipping into Parminder's cage, a flat wooden spoon in his firm grip?

•

So, the strategy I've been experimenting with takes place in the space between writing and then writing again. It happens, I guess, in the notebook that accompanies writing, which is never seen. About three weeks ago, I opened my notebook and placed it next to a manuscript I'd recently completed, about which I felt a subtle and persistent sense of shame. I was ashamed because it took me so long to write, that I hadn't really managed being the mother of a young child and writing productively at the same time, and I was ashamed, too, because nothing seemed to happen in the book itself. Instead, recursively, the

---

I know. Is she here?

Winter refuses to be allegorical. Where are my witnesses?
(La règle du jeu)　　　　No.　　　　　　　*(La règle du jeu)*
(La règle du jeu)　　　　She didn't come?　*(La règle du jeu)*
(La règle du jeu)　　　　Is she here?　　　*(La règle du jeu)*
They rented horse-drawn carriages and hung all the horses

　　with flowers. Children sang in the streets, frightened men in showers.
　　　　(La règle du jeu)(La règle du jeu)(La règle du jeu)
　　　　(La règle du jeu)(La règle du jeu)(La règle du jeu)(La règle du jeu)
　　　　(La règle du jeu)(La règle du jeu)(La règle du jeu)(La règle du jeu)
　　　　(La règle du jeu)(La règle du jeu)(La règle du jeu)(La règle du jeu)
　　　　　　　(La règle du jeu) 6 mo is the average, *(La règle du jeu)*
　　　　　　　　　　　　　　　　　　　　　　　　　　　I know.
　　　　　　but given my condition and general health I could
　　　　　　　　　　　　　　　　　　　　　　　　　　　No.

more depressing. In an article published in the *Poker*, Steve Evans analysis of prize-earnings from 1998-2004 counted 919 women prize-winners, and 854 men.

wolfgirls I was writing of found themselves—recursively, obsessively—straining against the gelatin envelope that enclosed the architecture of the jungle, and later the township they were taken to, discovered then captured by a Mission priest. I not sure why I did this, but it was both an antidote to the agitation of not really knowing what it was I had written, of not being able to say I had written a work of fiction, and also a re-orientation, of myself, and what I had written, to desire. I decided, in short, to translate what I had written as an index of the straining, pulsing movements the two girls made—in incipience, in the red cave beneath the floor of the jungle, in their clarified or violently restricted captivity, and in a fairytale of my own imagination. I looked for places where the composure or outline of the figure I was writing became blurry, or altered, in any sense, and then I tracked what was set in motion. I noticed that these "motions" or acts were sometimes permitted and sometimes curtailed. I wasn't interested in that. I wrote, instead, a set of lines analogous to the lines a body made, as it tried to enter the jungle or split it, caught in the branches of the perimeter—irrespective of the event of domestication, the narrative of capture. These lines are so minimal and simple when I look at them, basic, but I felt an inexpressible happiness when I wrote them, rapidly and with the kind of joy that

---

go much much longer...a year, year and
(La règle du jeu)(La règle du jeu)(La règle du jeu)(La règle du jeu)(La règle du jeu)(La règle du jeu)(La règle du jeu)(La règle du jeu)(La règle du jeu)(La règle du jeu)(La règle du jeu)(La règle du jeu)(La règle du jeu)(La règle du jeu)(La règle du jeu)(La règle du jeu)(La règle du jeu)(La règle du jeu)(La règle du jeu)
(La règle du jeu)(La règle du jeu)
(La règle du jeu)(La règle du jeu)   No.
(La règle du jeu)
(La règle du jeu)(La règle du jeu)(La règle du jeu)(La règle du jeu)
(La règle du jeu)(La règle du jeu)(La règle du jeu)
(La règle du jeu)(La règle du jeu)   *(La règle du jeu)*
half...but that eventually She didn't come? She couldn't make it. But I did it all for her! Elsewhere, is what I wanted to say, some place where cold beer is served on warm wooden tables, where the tree frogs hit the window and it is only June where people come in peated platoons and pay with strict attention. Where allus lies over all of us, where there are two bridges and no noses, where

However, when only prizes paying $1000 or more were counted, 645 men received $9,365,262, or an average of $14,520 per man, while 709 women

makes you forget that you haven't figured out what to do in any other part of your life. I offer them here, as a template of translation, and also as a wish, for the writing and desire to come, in your life as much as mine:

I wrote her going in.
I wrote her emerging from the under-spaces of the jungle floor.
I wrote her inside those real spaces, twitching, in an incomplete,
   lunar darkness.
I wrote her walking in.
I wrote her capture in the beak of the wolf.
I wrote human capture.
I wrote her on the other side, obsessed with the perimeter.
I wrote her walking out, caught in the branches of the perimeter.
I wrote her straining against the gelatin membrane of the jungle,
   distended in appearance for the animals within.
I wrote her in the garden, banking at the edge.
I wrote her attempted escape.
I wrote her as a soul, slipping between the bars of the Home.
I wrote her sister into the body of a bird.

---

the Black Prince won, where my brother is no longer *something* I know.
will
emerge...
noise noise no noise, love no hated love, no farther droppered dose, so so *so I coast.* Undo this button, I'll done the rest.

(La règle)(du jeu)

received $7,049,017, or an average of $9,942 per woman. So, 53% of the over $1000 prizes are won by women, but they only win 43% of the money. // One of

I wrote her in a grave, still available as a presence.
I felt her heart with my hand through the dirt.
I looked into her eyes in the bathroom mirror.
There, I saw another child, a boy, reflected in her eyes,
 doubling the narrative.
Then I went to India and wrote, in a jungle of sal. I said it was sal.
I wrote at a table in the jungle, as if alone, but illuminated by hurricane
 lamps and candles, for the film.
I wrote rubbish, keeping my hand moving for the camera.
I wandered away from the shot and wrote there, where other images and
 stories proliferated.
I wrote for seven years, obsessively returning to a site of capture, of
the image of a girl drenched in a dark pink fluid, caught in the branches
 of the jungle.
I wrote, imagining that writing was the emergent act, the gesture that
gave this image a destiny.
But it wasn't.

Somagraph
Meiling Cheng

A prominent theme that endures through the many beginnings in "The Laugh of the Medusa" is Cixous's call for "writing the body." While she repeats the theme frequently in the abstract, she also embodies it in textual practice by transfusing her essay with meticulous descriptions of bodily sensations, as if to swaddle her reader in a somatic blanket of feminine eroticism. Her body, verbalized and scrupulously transcribed, becomes so deeply woven into her text that I propose to call her writing a somagraph, a written account that purports to represent the body, seemingly through a grafting of the senses onto the text. *L'écriture féminine* bearing the signature of Hélène Cixous is a phenomenal somagraph, giving gender and sexuality a free hand to paint on the canvas of corporeality.

The concept of somagraph highlights the affinity between Cixous's feminine writing and the majority of feminist performances that emerged in the decade Cixous began publishing her avowedly female-sexed texts. Their similarities

Ashton's undocumented claims is that women make up half the faculties of creative writing programs. We could not find any well-done study of gender and

•

In January 2007, a real girl, Rochom, a jungle presence, walked out of a jungle in Cambodia, where she was found by woodcutters and restrained: a feral self, scarred but intact, and saying this, again and again, as she strained to get back to the trees: "Father, mother, stomach-ache."
    I wrote a correlative cut. I made a cut in the sal and let my wolfgirl emerge, blinking, into the dazzling light.
    I wrote the convergent image, one that exists in two places at once, and then I was done.
    I wrote in a gestural duration, mimicking the blankness of capture at different points.
    I did not know that writing like this would mean, for my own life, a radical new way of being in the world.
    I wrote until I was in the world.
    I sent my book into the world.

---

are so striking that Cixous's essay appears inadvertently as a testimonial to the predominant strategies of feminist body art since the 1970s. These strategies include the assertion of authorial gender identity, the naming of women as the intended spectatorial constituency, the use of a creative medium to stake a claim in cultural history, and the choice of the artist's female-identified body as the site of insurgence and contestation. Among these strategies, the use of the female body has met the strongest disapproval from feminist critics.[1] Instead of replicating their well-argued critiques here, I am interested in linking "The Laugh of the Medusa" with feminist performance to continue my speculation of whether Cixous's body-based feminine writing still holds enabling potentials for writers today.

•

Cixous's feminine writing shares feminist body art's reclamation of the female body as a legitimate source and subject matter for creative expression. Having anointed writing as her privileged vehicle to access and carry the cultural capital, Cixous pinpoints the body as the geography that her writing will map, if also invent.

creative writing faculty. We tried to produce some numbers ourselves but were stymied by several factors. One is that it is impossible to tell who is an adjunct

RAPE
Wanda Coleman

i am here to help you. and his partner laughed. she squeezed
her palms/triggers. their uniforms bled
the laughter became screams of horror and she
dragged the bodies of the white blond cop and
his Chinese bunky downstairs
and buried them in her eyes/hatred
sprang up and blossomed

talk about it

tell me every detail, said the doctor
they broke in on me. every detail. they took me
in the bedroom, one at a time. next detail

"Censor the body and you censor breath and speech at the same time," declares Cixous, who turns the task of writing into a liberatory act, while claiming the body to be what must be heard, emancipated, and rewritten. The "body" under Cixous's authorship is an entity poised between the specific and metaphorical. The Cixousian body, while individualized as her own, keeps transgressing its particular enfleshed boundary to touch what the writer considers the universal aspects of womanhood: her gendered corporeality, inexhaustible sexuality, and maternity. Although I cannot embrace Cixous's totalizing claims here, I do find myself drawn to the almost careless abandon of her poetic reveries, which allow the possibility of empathy to override the rigor of disciplined argument.

No matter her writing's reductive tendency, Cixous's attention to embodiment reflects her belief in the female body as a fundamental material base for tracing the sociocultural inscriptions of femininity. Cixous's devotion to transcribing the sensuous female experiences to written texts serves her purpose of exposing the artificial limit of gender construction. Cixous's corporeal pursuit also indicates her attempt to tap into the unconscious as a vital source of writerly imagination. Janet Wolff has argued that the "body has been systematically repressed and

and who is a tenure-line faculty on many of the creative writing faculty lists that are available on the web, and women tend to be disproportionally represented

i was scared they'd find my purse—i lied about
having no money. detail, detail. they undressed me,
asked me to tell them how it felt. did it feel
good? yes. did you cum? they were gentle lovers
did you cum? yes. both times? yes

the boyfriend

came in. she was feeling shrunken dirty suicide
she hadn't douched. the wetness still pouring
out/a sticky rivulet on her inner thighs
he got indignant. why didn't she call the police
why didn't she call her mama. why didn't she die
fighting. she remained silent. he asked her where
it happened. she showed him the spot. he
pulled down his pants, forced her back onto the sheets
i haven't cleaned up, she whined. but he was
full saddle hard dicking and cumming torrents

---

marginalized in Western culture, with specific practices, ideologies, and discourses controlling and defining the female body. What is repressed, though, may threaten to erupt and challenge the established order."[2] Cixous shares Wolff's feminist investment in corporeality as a key to unlocking the repressed and debased values in the hegemonic binaries, especially those between mind and body, masculinity and femininity. "The Laugh of the Medusa" not only addresses the "lesser" terms in these reified dichotomies, but does so through a rhetoric route paved with contradictions. At times Cixous repudiates binarism. She asserts that writing the body is "working (in) the in-between" (84), in a fluctuating interstice energized by bisexuality, which exists, in gradations of difference, within each person, male or female. At other times, Cixous espouses the preexisting dichotomy, only to exacerbate it by exulting the suppressed terms. *"In body,"* she exclaims, "more so than men who are coaxed toward social success, toward sublimation, women are body. More body, hence more writing" (87). Without pausing to contemplate the dubious identification of women with body, Cixous holds the condition of gendered embodiment as the impulsion for women to write.

in adjunct lines. However, we can mention a very well done (although it does not provide separate data for creative writing faculty) 2006 AAUP study that

the two burglars

kicked the door in. she woke. she thought, he's
drunk again. she slipped into her thin pink
gown, got up and went to see. it wasn't him. we
have guns, the dark one announced
there's no one here but me and the kids she said

there was little

for them to steal. the dark one took her into
the bedroom while his partner searched. he turned
out the lights and stripped. he laid her gently on
the bed. this is my name. when you cum, call
my name. she agreed. and he entered. your pussy's
hot and tight. where's your old man? he's a fool
not to be here with you. you're pretty

•

But why does a woman's gendered embodiment deserve such uninhibited enthusiasm? Cixous justifies her case by assuming the innate value of femininity, which she regards as the corporeal wellspring for women's sexuality and maternity. In Cixous's treatment, sexuality and maternity are both glorious expressions of life. While cautioning against classifying female sexuality into homogeneous codes, Cixous settles on interrelated geo-spatial tropes to describe femininity as the sexuality that is pan-erotogeneous, infinite, torrential, cosmic, filled with adventurous "trips, crossings, trudges," and traversing a "thousand and one thresholds of ardor" (86). "Woman for women" (83): Cixous gifts her body, textualized in her rhapsodic feminine writing, to other women, encouraging them to do the same: "Write your self. Your body must be heard." (81)

Insofar as Cixous relates sexuality to subjectivity and to writerly agency, she links female sexuality more with autoeroticism than with sexual consummation between partners. Thus, her gift to other women more closely resembles that of a mother who gives bodies to her daughters than that of a lover who expects

concluded that despite women earning more than half of all graduate degrees conferred, they still are underrepresented among tenured and tenure-track

you're soft. you fuck good. kiss me. and she did
as told. we don't want to hurt you. you like
the way i kiss. tell the truth. it's good,
she said and after a while she moaned his name

the other one

came in and took off his clothes in the dark
i'm really sorry to do this, he said, but
i can't help myself. strange, she thought. such
polite rapists. i wonder if they'll kill me?
somehow i must make them care enough not
to kill me. he told her his name and sucked
hungry at her nipples, parted her legs
he was very thick long hard. his friend's seed
eased the pain. i want your tongue he said
give me your tongue. she gave and gave

---

erotic gratification in return. With a unilateral passion that gives without being asked, Cixous plunges her readers, her discursive progeny, into an incarnated existence, even as she alerts them to the pleasure, beauty, violence, intricacy, and complexity of embodiment. Similar to what she has done with Medusa, Cixous appropriates—or has stolen back, as she would have put it—a trope most revered and troubled by the masculinist regimes of representation to make "the mother" a metaphor for the life-giving, body-endowing love. If she is at fault here for essentializing "woman" as an always already altruistic maternal body, she does so to dislocate "womanhood" and "maternity" from their conceptual subjugation as coerced accomplices to patriarchy. By reframing these signifiers within a context inclusive of female desire, she refashions both notions to be creative forces in a gender politics that rebukes the denigration of women.

•

Being a somagraph, "The Laugh of the Medusa" may be read as a pregnant text that contains within its locus many embryonic repercussions from feminist body art. However, I argue, Cixous's somagraph actually ends where feminist body art

faculty members. The study notes four things about the year 2005-2006: 1) nationally, women constituted 39 percent of full-time professors, 48 percent of

Jesus! he cried and shot into her, long spastic jerks
he trembled and fell into her arms. shit
that was good

in the kitchen

her few valuables were piled neatly mid-floor
she promised not to call the police
what could they do, save her?
the other one, the Jesus-man took her typewriter
and put it back, and all the other stuff they
had planned to take, even the television

here is my number, said the dark one
when you get lonely, call
and she walked

---

begins. Although she vows to take her body as a source and model of her writing, Cixous's finished artwork is the text, not the body. Inversely, feminist body art takes the woman artist's body as the starting point of an event. The body, however it's treated during performance, is also the resulting artwork. This corporeal artwork can only begin the process of becoming a somagraph, with culturally intelligible pertinence, when it manages to generate discursive circulation subsequent to its enactment. Whereas Cixous's feminine writing and feminist body art share similar intents, the differences in their chosen mediums mark them apart.

Cixous's somagraph exemplifies her approach to writing the body. A flesh counterpart of somagraph, feminist body art may be construed as a kind of body writing, being a performative action committed by a live body and projecting an open set of narratives about its *raison d'être*. Writing the body results in a piece of writing; body writing, which is ultimately flesh not text, nurses the hope of inspiring some future actions that may write the body. The subtle shift between "writing the body" and "body writing" reflects the more ontological distinction between writing and body. This distinction, in turn, hints at the limit of both endeavors.

the part-timers; 2) women held 44.8 percent of tenure-track positions and only 31 percent of the tenured positions; 3) women held on average just 24 percent of

them to the door. the dark one took her in his arms
kissed her goodbye

she waited

until she was sure they wouldn't
come back and kill

she picked up the phone

and made the mistake of thinking the world
would understand.

    Cixous's somagraph faces the conundrum of cross-media representation, since she employs a symbolic system to approach a live entity that, for all its symbolic constructedness, does have a somatic materiality that exceeds discursive representation. This conundrum finds a different manifestation in feminist body writing, where the artist's body stands as a visual stimulus that invites and awaits interpretation. Without subsequent discursive articulation, the body as writing is opaque—if not unreadable, at least equivocal in its multiplicity. This double-edged conundrum reveals the extent of difficulty in transferring information between literary and visual representations, between writing the body and body writing. Cixous's action of writing the body takes place in a discursive field, which employs a relatively permanent medium of printed letters. Accordingly, "The Laugh of the Medusa" may exist indefinitely as a somagraph, persuading its readers of its significance in feminist liberation. By using a live medium, feminist body art aspires to present a breathing evidence of that significance in an immediate interactive environment. Yet, conditioned by its medium's transient liveness, body art suffers from the same destiny attending every living being: mortality. A body writing, which happens only once in performance,

full professorships; 4) female professors earned on average just 81 percent of what men earned. // There are some huge limitations around our methods of

Unreliable Witness
Chris Kraus

There is a recurring belief that certain decisions were made for us while we were still lost in the womb of our childhoods. Transactions were brokered in windowless rooms. Armies of people speaking in bland West Coast American accents. Audio tapes washed up at a yard sale. Always, the real story was elsewhere. Las Vegas, Nevada. Phoenix and Tempe. What were the voices describing? A carton of water-stained books found in an old man's garage. Proliferation of data surpassed proliferation of nuclear warheads. Old metal, junked electronics. Dictation equipment. Deposing as testament. The sloppiness of all this. Political porn.

Two years ago when my hearing dropped off I met someone who wanted to kill me. Death had drawn me a few times before but I always invented something to do. Running and stumbling. Hitchhiking on the Post Road outside Bridgeport, Connecticut to New Haven to hear the Black Panthers speaking at Yale, a man with a gun picked me up. I was 12 or 13 and school bored me immeasurably. I had the sense there was some other game to be entered at a very

---

completes itself by utter self-consumption; its corporeal vehicle renders its very composition vulnerable to the expenditure of time. A body writing invests in the capacity of memory to transmit its influence, for it relies on subsequent discursive articulations—by the artist and/or by other witnesses—to establish the artwork's wider cultural efficacy, while facilitating its transformation into written memories.

•

For its accessibility to the history of published records, writing the body seems to have an edge over body writing. "The Laugh of the Medusa," for instance, is simultaneously a piece of feminine writing and a historical record, whereas any body artwork must depend on documentation to enter art history. Out of writing the body emerges a textual product, which enjoys the endorsement from the existing cultural hierarchy that places the permanent above the ephemeral, writing above the body, implicitly gendering the former as male/masculine and the latter female/feminine. It is precisely against such hierarchical valuation that Cixous proposes to write the body, refusing to separate the two entities to

collecting numbers. Still, what we found upset and confused us. We had thought Ashton was right. And that all that we had to argue was that she wasn't reading

high level. Traffic was glinting around us, it was still May but already hot. He said Open the glove-box, I have something to show you. I asked him a question, he said, Just do as I say. The gun was still in its box. He said, I want you to touch it. Slowly getting the point, I opened the box and ran my fingers along the aluminum barrel down to the handle. Ohhh, I said, It's so shiny and big. Now can we put it away?

Pussy smokes a cigarette, pussy blows smoke—penis exfoliation shaved pussy stories Nathan Sassover penis extraction Nathan Sassover litigation mediacom pretty women with cocks worldcast net Albany sex protein diets property management lingerie sale… The search-engine log of a website based in Romania. When I researched the killer online I had the sense something was looking over my shoulder, a primitive counting machine buried inside the circuit board. This turned out to be true.

There is a recurring belief that to locate this, this margin of error, would be to trace a historiography of one's present amnesia. Can no longer remember a time before the person stopped being part of the process. There were hallways leading to multiple doors. Behind them: a basketball court, loudspeakers, coaxial wires.

---

the extent of asserting the body as what originates her writing. Her subversion goes further as to claim writing for women; *écriture féminine* strips writing of its traditional male gender to make it possible for women to feminize this medium. For similar reasons, some women artists have chosen the medium of performance, turning to their bodies as the material and instrument of subversion. The lack of permanence that epitomizes both the body and the performance event constitutes the body writing's feminist appeal as a defiant gesture against expropriation by hegemonic interest.

Despite the numbing whispers of our cultural habit, we must recognize that permanence is not necessarily superior to transience. There is certainly more than one form of death. Although I've argued that "The Laugh of the Medusa" may continue to renew its textual body through the exchange with different readers, there is no guarantee that its information will not become outdated, having outlived its purpose in a linguistic stasis. In fact, the binary terms that support Cixous's essay, including "woman," "man," "feminine," "masculine," "self," "other," and "mother," have all been undergoing radical inquiry at our posthuman and transgendered moment. In this renewed context, feminist body

the data correctly. But we're not so sure anymore. We're fairly convinced she is wrong; that things haven't been that great since the mid-'80s. // And then we

Instruments used for conversion. Set theories in which the system eventually takes over. Behind the doors there is only one room.

The killer needed my money. Since others were already taking my money and not giving much in return, this seemed like a sublime and radical move. He had a highly developed imagination... a background in neuromedical research combined with the creation of Music and a strong interest in visual arts... a life balance achieved from a multitude of creative pursuits, verifiably accomplished... He used that word, 'verifiable,' the first time we spoke. Later, I'd learn more about the verification of lies, the way a set of fundamentally false assertions could metastasize across the web. The mirror effect of simulation: websites and vanity posts in trade publications, patents with long numbers pending but never approved, blog entries, infomercials broadcast on space-rental domains, fabulations that check out against themselves.

Age management therapeutics for a new generation of health care Nuranex a groundbreaking new category Not a prescription drug or an ordinary supplement but a unique formula If you experience feelings of fatigue irritability or mood swings Get a 30 day supply

---

writing has the advantage of being able to evolve and change in a faster and more fluid pace; its enfleshed opacity makes it much more adaptable to the paradigmatic shifts in the overall epistemic environment. More chimerical than its textual double, body writing can more readily direct how writing the body may resonate with the current agendas in feminist liberation, even as it challenges what "feminism" means and means to do.

My point of comparing Cixous's feminine writing with feminist body art is not to oppose these two practices, but to underscore their complementary contributions to what, I believe, we may still call the women's movement. Producing somagraphs remains relevant to this movement, not just for its express claims in subverting the hegemonic ideology, but also for its productive vulnerability, its susceptibility to feminist critique itself, that serves to keep the movement ever vigilant.

asked ourselves, should we care? And what number is the right number? Should all anthologies be 50% women? Should all prizes? Does it matter if women are

We met at the Chateau Marmont—this was real. We ordered glasses of wine. We were both overdressed. We discovered we both liked the word delirium. He was empathetic to the particular challenge to submissive women trapped in their rational head about the recurring enlarging need for surrender and loss of control. I saw him see my unhappiness. I felt it lift out of my body and enter his eyes. He had this capability. He had interests in media properties he had acquisitions he had patents for the remote keyless entry device he was launching research initiatives in conjunction with doctors he was helping humanity he was opening residential facilities for clinical trials he was releasing a 3-disc CD of original electronic piano performed and mastered himself.

Minutes after my unhappiness entered his head, I noticed his right eye started to twitch. When we left the Chateau I got my car from the valet garage. His—a black BMW—was parked up the hill on the road. Truth is an experiment we are always conducting. He said he did not want it scratched. Pushed to extremes, the machines become each other's prostheses. Which one was generative, which one receives? Changes in language both reflect and enforce a reduction in consciousness. Collateral damage, prisoner abuse. Compound nouns twice removed.

Works Cited:

1. See, for examples: • Laura Mulvey. "Visual Pleasure and Narrative Cinema." *Visual and Other Pleasures*. Bloomington: Indiana University Press, 1989. 14-28. • Griselda Pollock. *Vision and Difference: Femininity, Feminism, and the Histories of Art*. London: Routledge, 1988. Regarding critiques of écriture féminine, see: • Gayatri Spivak. "French Feminism in an International Frame." *In Other Worlds*. New York: Methuen, 1987. 134-153. • Ann Rosalind Jones. "Writing the Body: Toward an Understanding of l'Écriture féminine" (1981). *Feminisms: An Anthology of Literary Theory and Criticism*, ed. Robyn R. Warhol and Diane Price Herndl, Revised Edition. New Brunswick, NJ.: Rutgers University Press, 1997. 370-383.

2. Janet Wolff. "Reinstating Corporeality: Feminism and Body Politics." *The Feminism and Visual Culture Reader*, ed. Amelia Jones. London: Routledge, 2002. 415.

not very well represented in some of this stuff? And because we could think of so many successful feminist achievements, we found that we ourselves felt the

He asked if I'd like to surrender control of my assets to him. When I played the CDs his piano performance—flawless technique used to hold back an imminent chaos—evoked someone I knew.

Together, we drew up a table of contents:

ACCEPTANCE AND SELF-ACCEPTANCE
AFFIRMATION: SEE SELF-TALK
AGGRESSION: SEE ASSERTIVENESS
ANIMA AND ANIMUS
ARCHETYPES
ARCHETYPAL FIELDS
ARCHETYPAL FIELD WORK
AS-IF PRINCIPLE
ATTACHMENT
SEE: FORMS OF ATTACHMENT: SEEKING CONNECTIVITY
CERTAINTY: THE FLUID NATURE OF CERTAINTY

Sexspace
Dodie Bellamy

When he read her first message his heart leapt. *Hmm. She's not capitalizing her name, hmm, she's open, her guard's down, seducible.* He hurled a message back at her, "Ooh! that's some sexy fuckin alliteration." And it occurred to him that he might be falling in love with language. He imagined a woman typing, the absolute physicality of her fingers twitching out words, her cunt beneath the keyboard vivid and slimy as a totally ripe persimmon his cock hardening her breasts above the keyboard heaving and bobbing. A woman writing email, he concluded, was impossibly erotic.

LC = LEISURE CLASS = LOCATE CLITORIS = LOAD OF COME = LAME CHRIST = LAP CUNT = LITTLE CHILD = LOW CUNT = LOWER CASE

Manifesto: Our universe is composed of three realms: sexspace, phonezone, and mere life. These three realms, or planes, exist simultaneously at different

continuing sexism of the experimental/postmodern/avant-garde/innovative writing scene somewhat easy to ignore; and also a little pathetic. Everything

He suggested we travel to Acapulco together. He was planning to open a clinic on the grounds of a former resort. I'd sign some papers. The list ended with 'W,' 'Worry.' I told myself, Don't.

Later on—thanks to a journalist friend who does espionage work for corporate America—I learned that he'd sold a house in Benedict Canyon six months before for $1.8 million but there was no money left. Lawsuits pending against him included two by his former attorneys… Spousal battery charges filed, then abruptly dropped, 2004… linked by various filings to a group of companies using the name Parasol… Parasol Group Parasol Media Parasol Entertainment … Parasol being a kind of umbrella used in hot climates… Pre-internet background in cable, production of porn… Unfulfilled notes against assets disposed of held by individuals linked to the Armenian mob… Legal address (200 square foot linoleum-floored commercial space) on 9000 block of Wilshire Boulevard shared by five unregistered companies to which he has ties… Possibly living out of his car… By this time, his twitch had entered my left eye.

Debriefing of subject proceeded as follows:

---

rates of vibration. Sexspace is the force that sustains all creation. In phonezone, sexspace vibrations are lower and denser. In mere life they're denser and lower still. Through extreme sexual obsession lovers can sex travel, raising their vibratory levels to link directly into sexspace. Sex travel is an ancient science that has been streamlined and updated for today's computer savvy public. Previously, the voluntary translation to another sphere has been the prerogative of the gods. Now through the internet anyone can learn to do it. Sexspace is a realm of pure tempered abstraction, there the fucking is without end. Sexspace is formless yet unlimited in formness, it can take any form or no form, there is no inside, no outside, no he she it me, in sexspace we are all genders, all sex, all species, animals and machines meld in the great prosthetic spasm. Sexspace is senseless in that no senses are involved. Desire leaps from form to form gleefully as swingers in '70s films leap from bed to bed. It is common for the flesh body, parked on a desk chair, to quake with orgasm. Sex travel is great for going to the dentist. A master of sexual bilocation has no need for novocaine, she can raise her vibratory level and leave her body prone on the dental chair as she frolics in sexspace my cock is twelve feet long, thick and jiggly as k-y jelly, my cock is a lovely translucent

from Kelsey Street to Pussipo (a listserv of 100+ experimental/postmodern/avant-garde/innovative women writers) showed us we could do what we wanted

When I met him it was as if he could see straight through me, beyond things that happened, back to my childhood. In his presence I could look through the past to a better more probable life. I saw what could have been.

He said: "Answer me. Answer me truthfully." But I couldn't do this. Pieces, excuses, falling away. He said: "You see? The truth is so very simple. Why do you have to give false answers to get to the true?"

He told me to follow, and I wanted this very badly. To be blasted. He spoke to the evidence: the variable nature of my present truth. When he noted the fragility of my current life-form, I felt his intelligence as something painful. To me and to him.

He promised to speak to the areas of puzzlement, protocol, ambiguity of thought beyond what was said. When you obscure the truth about your actual needs so do you intervene in your own progression. He said. He offered to teach me progressive devotion. The transformative nature of this can be trusted through each stage of the process. He said.

Since I wasn't going to give my money away, I decided to move it around and make more.

---

shimmer extending from my chest, it bends around corners, I trail after it, wide-eyed, throbbing.

Sexsutra: No space between two words, two bodies.

If she could step back in time, twelve or fifteen years—or even nine months ago—she would be inhabiting the thought processes of a stranger: Carla Moran, teacher, poet. She feels like the figment of someone else's imagination, but lacks the composite biography necessary to become that fiction. She feels like Arnold Schwarzenegger in that movie, like she was born fullgrown, her memories implanted with Ed's first email. He recruited her, initiated her into the ancient science of sex travel, and she ceased to live any life save what he dictated the smell of new rubber on his tennis shoes in those airways she lost her soul. When he shut down everything at once she had no inner resources, just this wracking realization: the master was a fraud, his love plagiarized from Lorca, the Kama Sutra, OS 8.6. Do the inner worlds exist? Will Ed abscond sex travel funds to buy condos in Hawaii? Left in the dark without a deprogrammer, she rambles

to do. And we distinctly remember thinking this when we were younger writers, trying to figure out what we could do. But all this possibility, born from a long

>   Another room remembered from childhood:
>   When I ran into Melanie's attic to hide from the boys I crouched behind magazines stacked up in boxes—*Reader's Digest, Scientific American, Playboy, Popular Mechanics, True Crime,* and *Tease*. Later I realized the magazines made up some kind of template or diagram of a future still being imagined. A future already part of the past. The magazines made up a code if you knew how to read. I think they belonged to her Dad. Outside Kenny was burning Nancy's hand with a cigarette. We were smoking Kool Menthols, she was tied to a tree, on some level this was ok. The radio played *Born To Be Wild*, all the girls wanted to do it. A red Pontiac Sunfire, a McDonalds. I was being poisoned by the culture then but I didn't know it. They were building the town's second mall.
>   Running away, 12 hours south to Bahia de los Angeles—a long dusty street —end of the road—2.18.05—slept 10 hours last night—panic about calling the broker—finally Lourdes lets me use the hotel phone for a long distance call—will net maybe 1.5 million—my left eye still has the twitch.

---

through the sex goddess' graveyard, surrounded by humans who ride bicycles, eat Kung Pao Chicken, kiss the air, talk—their actions inexplicable and wooden. She wishes she could blink her eyes and freeze the old ways forever. Beneath each door she spies a line of vivid turquoise light.

Even the most doctrinaire distance romance advocates will admit that human contact has its advantages. But if you can't get to a lover or are at a stage in life where physical contact no longer appeals, distance sex is a perfectly reasonable alternative. Indeed, while distance sex got its start as a compensation for "geographic disadvantage," its most enthusiastic audience has proven to be members of a demographic niche under-served by the current system: the lonely adult. The median age of a network lover is thirty-four. Half are married; two thirds have children; nine out of ten are lovers part-time. By and large they are people in an accountable place in life who wouldn't be able to get a lover in any other way.

Cultbuster: Like everyone else, Carla and Ed turned to sexspace when things weren't going right. Like everyone else, they found no salvation there, only

history of women publishing magazines and presses, of women starting listservs, couldn't really fix or address the other kinds of gender trouble we still dealt

What is Gender Today?
Eileen Myles

I'm thinking gender is a word that language used to need to operate. I say that cause it's the first time I heard the word maybe in high school latin, the time when the word gender made a dent. Because it's not like job applications ever used the word. They instead would say emphatically male female check one. There were only two rooms. But in latin gender made it be so words persistently had endings that belonged to one or another gender—like farmer. Agricola, agricolae. Latin made a choice that farmer was more female than male. And maybe they were saying that farming was female not the farmer. So that gender had something to do with the spirit and nature of things not people. And we have that in English in this other way. That ships are female. We could all make that list probably quickly so I won't bother. Feminism spawned some public consciousness about the gender biases in the English language which resulted perhaps in the huge result that we can now have male hurricanes once in a while. I don't think anyone actually gives a shit that Katrina was female rather

---

the limiting ramparts of twentieth-century romanticism. Oscillating between attraction and repulsion, sexspace functions as a subsonic suction cup that swallows happiness along with tragic complacencies. In sexspace fantasies are life forms. Sexspace absorbs these fantasies, grows consciousness from them, and takes their shape, bits of hell clinging to messages, Carla thinks Ed's her lover but really it's the SexThing assuming Ed's syntax, mouthing endearments, quoting Victor Hugo forever you are somehow touched with the dark. Simultaneously one and many, the SexThing is an ancient creature that, having survived so long and gulped down so many consciousnesses, believes it is god. As Ed caressed the keyboard demon after demon entered through his fingers, had been entering him for months, the molecules in his body moved apart for them and his flesh felt spongy, so much energy swirling through him. The SexThing was growing enormous, coalescing into a raggedy mountain of lust that loomed over his desktop his monitor torn and leaking, his words cracked faces with gouged eyeballs at this rate he was never going to fix the glitches in the DownWorld website, Donald was breathing down his neck about incompatibilities with Netscape, like whenever the dancing geese animation loaded the browser froze,

within experimental/postmodern/avant-garde/innovative poetry communities on a fairly regular basis, because the constant somewhat snide anti-feminist

than male. But I'm wondering if meteorologists have a compulsory pattern for assigning gender to storms. Every other storm has to be male something like that. I bet when they see a big one coming they revert to always calling it female. I can research this but I won't today but my guess is that a big violent storm will always be ours.

•

But who are we? We're changing. I'm on a plane and every now and then I hear a cat meow. Meowup. It's like a drink. An invitation. And we're someone that that makes a little hot. I'll have to get up at some point and find the cat and say hello. It will be a warm exchange undoubtedly because no matter what we look like our affirmation of the cat's adorableness will be a gateway to an ungendered space of almost musical affection between larger mammals. That would be my utopian ideal for gender and I go there first in writing before I anticipate it in the world, but I discover it in the world as a feeling I'd like to relocate someplace else. It swaps I guess in my utopian gendered imaginary which is my writing. An intimate tone is immediately allowed around cats and

---

tech support was receiving dozens of disgruntled emails about it a day, what a bunch of fucking losers, what kind of geek would waste their time online looking at down comforters, anyway, the kind who are losers enough to write whiny emails, what he really should do is break the link to the "contact us" button, let those down-sucking losers really sit there and stew. Ed's therapist gave him a vial of genetically-altered bacteria, which he dashed against his keyboard, the tiny gulped the immense and the SexThing crumbled into a million gleaming black sexchunks light as charcoal. Ed stopped emailing Carla. The geese would dance again.

Sexsutra: The act is a species of person.

Carla stands behind the egg yolk yellow strip that edges the subway platform, a foot and a half wide, the strip is bumpy and rubbery, she imagines the rubbery bumps are for blind people, so they can feel the edge and won't totter into the pit of tracks—or maybe it's simply because everybody finds bumpy rubbery things repulsive and thus are less likely to teeter on the brink of the platform like one

rants and comments that define that scene to this day felt more troubling than the unequal numbers in anthologies and prize monies. And at the same time we

dogs. Check. Save. We know that and we exploit it for our own fellow feelings as we move through the world. A pet place is a gender free space and you'll find a lot of so called gender deviants gravitating around this tonal truism. A cute pet is like a pool. It's a water fountain. I suppose I wanted to distract myself in to this safe place instead of venturing further in the small exploration I'm on. The deploying of we into the world to experience gender together in different ways on this panel for fifteen minutes. It's like a moderate sex club. A gender ride so to speak. I'm an avid follower of my own and other beings gender experiences outside the norm. It's actually the only gender experience I know and though I could probably choose to write from the position of a married heterosexual woman, or a gay man in his sexual prime pre aids, roaming along the docks one night in 1973. I could inform my reader through my possession of a fine forty something phallus that had produced three kids already and got aroused on business trips by young women or men, but tamed that impulse by having a very nice clean young hooker up to my room to blow me. I like to drink a beer and ignore her and watch teevee until I completely explode in her face. I don't know what my wife does when I go away and I'm more comfortable that way.

---

of those twiggy toy birds that dips its beak in a glass of water, mesmerized by our own precarious rocking as the train comes racing forward. The drivers don't drive them. Computers do. The drivers read newspapers and sometimes, to Carla's horror, stand up and fidget with something behind their seats, their backs to the windshield as she plummets through darkness. Suspended above the platform a series of LED tickertapes deliver a continuous stream of warnings and announcements, red dot letters flash that in three minutes an Embarcadero train will arrive to hurl her, again, though these clattering mechanical bowels. Her flesh is such a delicate packet—pinkish membrane on the outside, inside wisps of capillaries, wet. Smashable as a mosquito. The tunnels remind her of sexspace—fuckable impulses clanging through thousands of miles of circuitry, it's noisy inside those wiry veins, a deafeningly high-pitched whir and a terrible humming—her love pleas to Ed arrive frazzled, in need of a stiff drink. "I love you," the screen shouts, bug-eyed, clothes rumpled, cigarette dangling dejectedly from lips.

had to admit, we sort of agree with Ashton about the limits of the single gender anthology. No one in the experimental/postmodern/avant-garde/innovative

Not knowing. But sometimes when I watch my kids play I think of the cum all over that girls face and run into the bathroom to jerk off and then I'm home. Do you think that's weird. And this is my gender isn't it, whether I think about these women and men when I write or when I'm having sex. I would welcome anyone who lived their life in a seemingly normal way to define themselves as gender queer which sounds like a permanent kind of arrival to me. And I do think we all are that when we coo around a pussy with total strangers but mostly one wouldn't own that. But you feel it, right? And one settles down too a little as time moves on. The first time we were told in 1965 with our Sassoon haircut to get out of the ladies room at the bowling alley and we had to assert that we were female and were humiliated and didn't want our girlfriends to know we had been taken for a boy but of course they always knew we were male somehow. The world I think anticipates your gender before you do. I think finally gender is a public thought. So when we went for long stretches in our teens and twenties as a successful heterosexual female and our dirty secret was that we were "not normal" that was all the inside of that performance could bear, that tiny fearful notion quivering, waiting for its solo, going out to play yet the inner feeling is

---

CM = CUNT MOTION = CAT MIMIC = CHRIST MONGER = COPULATES WITH MALES = CRIMINAL MIND = COCK MASTURBATOR = CUM MAGNET = CRUCIFIED MAMMAL = CARLA MORAN

poetry scene writes in a single gender space. And often the poetry collected in these anthologies is not saying that much about feminism or gender. And finally,

future gender performance and it was not until years later now NOT when we are wearing a top coat and a suit jacket and men's shoes in New York going to SVA to substitute teach for Ann Rower or Joan Schenkar and the bus driver calls us sir and we don't want to respond, we just don't know how to allow that public performance even though we are shaping it and doing the bidding of some inner fashion designer that knows that we can only teach as a man that that's where our authority lies though we are entirely open, proud about the fact that we are also and maybe in the latin agricola way female we are farming somehow, that is our feminism, we are willing to allow that the world, my name for instance, my birth, is female, we haven't adjusted that, but what the birth has carried all its life is often mostly some version of male but the bus driver perversely or simply wanted the man to DO something to take a ticket and we couldn't turn around and perform that bidding because surely someone else on the bus would probably see us different and we would be in danger then caught in the midst of two performances one true and one false and we were paralyzed so he stopped the damn bus until the freak came up and took a transfer. You know what it was: because we hadn't yet had a nice relaxed inner handshake with the

---

I Am Madam
Vanessa Place

I do not make selves. I make objects. My objects are swollen or slenderized, containing more or less of what may be taken for a singularity. Like sound with silence, the more sound, the less silence, more silence, less sound. Like sculpture, the more marble, the less space, more space, less marble. In this way, the largest sculptures are also the smallest, as they leave less space, for a sculpture is composed of the space of the carved stone and the space carved by the stone. So every symphony is smaller than Cage's *4'33"*, Mount Rushmore minute next to Giacometti. In music, the object is sound, the subject silence. In sculpture, the object is space, the subject time. The textualized subject is an temporal object. I make literal variations on objects that take up more or less space, sometimes spatially, on the page, like a sculpture, sometimes temporally, in the mind, like a sound. The thickness of these objects can be modulated by employing more or less realism and abstraction. Realism is metonymic, abstraction metaphoric.

we are not sure the single-gender anthologies are doing that much to "fix" the gender trouble. They certainly do not seem to be changing the gender spreads of

man inside he just couldn't do something so mundane as walk back up to the front of the bus and get a transfer—he couldn't be obedient. I think of this kind of gender performance—that one puts on the dog of another gender for pleasure or nature or whatever but hasn't planned to do any kind of public handshake with officialdom—for me this is drag or travesty, not deep. This might be insulting to someone but I think of it as playful. It's not literally changing your identity with drugs surgery or a committed passing all the time to finally even make the change in your wallet, on your id, and on the form too. You haven't checked male and moved away from your birth name. You haven't changed your passport—will I, will I? With the passage of time the aloneness with gender the mystery of going through menopause say with gender am I the oldest women here no there's a few of us who may or may not discover ourselves to be something else again we may have wanted to have sex with a man or become one. Then that passes too and returns. Writing hormones is that gender? I think hormones are writing don't you. And now when we return our cable box on 23rd st. in Manhattan and the man behind the counter asks us if the account is in our wife's name, and I smile and laugh and say no that's me and the man goes sorry but it's gentle because

---

Realism is fragmentary, chaotic, the illogic of as-is. Abstraction is globular, figured, the logic of willed-being. Abstraction is a martyr, realism the AM/PM. By altering my densities via narrative and abstraction, employing formalisms or chance or whatever else I palette, I make spotted objects that permit more or less entry while obliterating, like an inseminate egg, any real divide between insides. The read text like the soft nub of hard sense, like skin cut, put to cut skin, like color bled into canvas and words made weeping flesh, the rind that's supposed to keep you out and me in does not hold, but will stretch and fold, swell and split.

•

After Christmas, she could not leave the apartment: she did not have keys to go out, and he took the keys and telephone with him when he left. He chained her hands and feet before he went to work in the morning, her hands behind her, her legs sometimes together. He locked the chain to the bars on the kitchen window, locking her inside the apartment from 10:00 a.m. until he came home

anthologies. But at the same time, it is not that the single gender anthology is unnecessary because gender equality has been reached, rather it is that the

it's clear we meant to look this way and nature the writing of the hormones is supporting the performance for the first time the inside feels calm and we can joke man to man which makes the man less nervous I believe. I look around wondering what would a man do say when I'm trying to get a cab from LAX and a girl jumps in front of me to ask some question and all the cab men surround her and I get pissed because I'm seeing the dudes surround the girl and I'm thinking I need a cab you fuckwads and would a man get mad. Which man am I? And how has gender delivered me here, where the farm is still female and the farmer is male. All I'm saying about writing and gender is that if writing is a negotiating of the inside all of the time and so is being and fashion and sex then it would be this one marvelous ribbon. Some stars along the way in writing are Millie Wilson she has her marvelous gendered piece in *The New Fuck You* or I just read fucking *Orlando*—I honestly found all that swirliness disturbing before so it seems now my man is a little girlie, a femme but I say it takes a real man to wear a dress or write that way. Or not.

---

at 7:00. She did not have access to food or a bathroom during that time, and there was no bucket for her to use if she needed to relieve herself. The windows were left open for fresh air, and the television was left on. She could not stand, but he put a blanket on the floor for her to lie on. Sometimes the front door would also be chained; it was kept locked from the outside. She asked him not to chain her up, but he said no. The chains were tight, and hurt. When he came home and unchained her, he would want to have sexual relations by force.

•

You are a stupid little twat who if she sucked enough cock might just get ahead —to conceptually diagram the crux of that sentence, would it be S+V+O or O+V+S or O+V+O or O^3? The object is subject to interpretation, pregnant with identity, identity times three, and playing the part of the terrible sparrow is the second person me. Like Elinor Antin's *Carving*, the less of me, the more of me, for me is the object that you see. In her writings on the impersonality of Pound and Eliot, Maud Ellman notes that the more a text revolves around a single

experimental/postmodern/avant-garde/innovative poetry scene needs a more radical feminism; a feminism that begins with an editorial commitment to

from Shorter Chaucer Tales, 2006
Caroline Bergvall

1.
The Host Tale

The fruyt of every tale is for to seye;
They ete, and drynke, and daunce, and synge, and pleye.
They soupen and they speke,
And drynken evere strong ale atte beste.
"Now lat us sitte and drynke, and make us merie,
And lat us dyne as soone as that ye may;
Lat us heere a messe, and go we dyn
The service doon, they soupen al by day;
And to the dyner faste they hem spedde,
and go we dyn
With hym to dyne

---

self, the more fragmentary that self appears; catharsis then institutes the final distillation of that pip of pure I eyed, the mystery of incarnation becoming the mystery of resolution, which is never more than perspective poured in stone, or the past perfected tense.

At the same time, there is a cannibalistic hunger for the possibility of metamorphosis, for the putty-colored transcendence of change through change. Whether we'd be monstrous saint or sublime animal, there's nothing more human than the desire to unbecome human, to transform our flesh upwards or down, like matter itself, it doesn't really matter, as long as there's movement. Charles Singleton's book on the structure of the *Commedia* argues that if there is no promise of our transubstantiation, how can we have anything but history? History, noted Valèry, primarily creates history, as things, Auden added, are thrown into being. And history, you will doubtless recollect, is what gods make and creatures suffer. So let us be the goddish we, throwing Being into Thing, like Medusa's single creeled head, and let us be creatured, like all Medusa's flickering heads, catching beings at the moment they are most alive and freezing them in our most mobile perception, like Medusa's sculpting head, like a selfless

equitable representation of different genders, races and classes, but doesn't end there; an editorial practice that might begin with equitable representation in

To come to dyner
And thus I lete hem ete and drynke and pleye,
But thus I lete in lust and jolitee
I lete hem, til men to the soper dresse.
They ete and drynke, and whan this hadde an ende,
Of mete and drynke,
And eten also and drynken over hir myght,
To eten of the smale peres grene.
They drynke, and speke, and rome a while and pleye,
Ordeyened hath this feeste of which I tolde
Go
to feste
at a kynges feeste
Each man woot wl that at a kynges feeste
Hath plentee, to the mooste and to the leeste
Arrayed for this feste in every wise
Whan he of wyn was repleet at his feeste,

---

portrait, like the villanelle of a home video, like a new-torn sadness, we will fabricate for ourselves blue and red objects rendered in the past conditional and present progressive, a world wrought in intaglio, a world of glottal events that have a gutbucket existence, where existence is a supple metaphor for existence, the allegorical equivalence of the two official translations of Exodus 3:14—*I am what I am / I am that I am*. In the aspired rose window, we are scoped and pent in the eye of *the*.

•

"Nonsense," said the crocodile, "I think you mean to say: 'if every day's this lovely, I must mean to stay.'" "I mean I mean to cross," said the lady. "Well, if that's what you mean, then by all means, get a cross," said the crocodile, "I suggest you stamp your foot and shake your fist at the sky." "How on earth will that help me cross?" asked the lady. "Oh, all the ladies do it," assured the crocodile, "it is the very image of a cross lady."

•

order to think about how feminism is related to something other than itself, in order to make writing that thinks about these things visible. // How to do this?

They fette hym first the sweete wyn,
And sende hym drynke,
And there he swoor on ale and breed,
With bread and chesse, and a good ale in a jubbe
Cheweth greyn and lycorys
With whete and malt
Both mele and corn
be it whete or otes,
For male and breed, and rosted hem a goos
That they han eten with thy stubbel goos
And beggeth mele and chese, or elles corn.
Instide of flour yet wol I yeve hem bren
Than maystow chese
Yif us a busshel whete, malt, or reye,
A goddes kechyl, or a trype of chese,
Bacon or beef,
Seynd bacoun, and somtyme an ey or tweye,

I am permanent in time as a landscape. My what and that are acts of ashen happiness, unsightly arguments composting the definite article or realistic touch, that as-is object that I subjectify, as well as the abstract portrait, the metaphor or internal relation excreted, and then there's content melted to form like Narcissus flowering at the shore. It is an American tradition to make art out of the cheapest and most commonplace object via the supreme alchemical efforts of genius; we do not cotton to gold, and wring heroes straight from homespun. In this, Duchamp became our greatest Rumpelstiltskin, reducing the process of art to production, and production to packaging, and packaging to critique, genius to egress. It is an American tradition to revere success, measured quarterly and spooned out with celebrity, success as egress. The self is the cheapest commodity, that barking pink-tipped thing we all have hanging on our hands, like Time and imminent death, a self we want to believe is ready-made or made-ready, our matter doesn't much matter for packaging purposes, and the self historically scripted or cast is the easily sellable self—the outside one that exists in mechanical opposition. Any mechanical opposition, whether it be male/female, I/not I, good/evil, for it is the fracture that confirms our ultimate organicism. And in this way, we also

We don't know. We still don't know. // Hoping to find an answer with help from others, we asked a question to members of the experimental/postmodern/avant-

The bacon was nat fet for hem,
And of youre softe breed nat but a shyvere,
And after that a rosted pigges heed
Milk and broun breed,
many a muscle and many an oystre,
A cake of half a busshel fynde
many a pastee
And eek the wyn,
The spices and the wyn is come anoon,
Of spicerie, of leef, and bark, and roote
Ther spryngen herbes, grete and smale,
The lycorys and cetewale,
    And many a clowe-gylofre,
And notemuge to putte in ale,
Wheither it be moyste or stale,
    And roial spicerye,

---

learned to perform the mirrored pas de deux of mechanical meldings, insisting to similarly silly degree that there was no ineffable thingness to us, that between I and I no difference lies, or at least no difference that cannot be undone, via sex surgery or more better comprehension. We've become flea-bit objects convulsed into being, dry-eyed as a nurse, stateless as a slave. And in this abject subjected state, we proclaim ourselves arbiter of objectivity, slendered to no exterior, vented without perforation, suspended in our servile disbelief. Unnetted, unclosed, unspun. Without, of course, objection.

    Skins are thin, sir, most can tear at the blade of a leaf, the scratch of a knife, or the cut of an eye. Yet it's a keeper, remains the same. Evermore and back again. Skin, sir, is the toughest of hides.

                  We are, *consummatum est*.

                                    If everything, then what.

•

Medusa's revenge is her coup d'eye, the frozen pond of her violet I, her single head seizing through its many other heads the slitted heads of many others. This is why Narcissus is her lazy twin, frozen in his glaze of how others see

garde/innovative poetry scene—We'd be curious if you can imagine some way
that poetry, or poetry communities (again, however you define the terms) might

And gyngebreed
And lycorys, and eek comyn,
So that men myghte dyne.
Bacus the wyn hem shynketh al aboute,
And broghte of myghty ale a large quart
And whan that each of hem had dronke his part
Now kepe yow fro the white and fro the rede,
Whan man so drynketh of the white and rede
fro the white wyn of Lepe,
This wyn of Spaigne crepeth subtilly
And thanne he taketh a sop in fyn clarree,
He drynketh ypocras, clarree, and vernage
Of spices hoote
Or else a draught of fresh-drawn, malty ale,
I hadde levere than a barel ale
Drynketh a draughte
drinken of this welle a draughte

---

him. Despair coils in the back of the throat and in the sunlit mystery of the mooted incarnation. Fat, we are, with history, and growing fatter, and the future of us lies in this thick past tense, but if we can keep ourselves eternally present, insisting on an absolute lack of interpretation or on the translation itself, then there is no getting around me, for I become undone all over again, carving down to the bare boneless of us. Because the present tense, you must agree, is unbearable in its narrative possibility.

During a Q & A, I asked a famous feminist art critic about aesthetics now, as the emphasis then was on making, particularly the making of history, and now that history's been made, what about the art? She said she did not think a lot about aesthetics. I think a lot about aesthetics. I asked another about the significance of narrative, why stories were so often embraided into women's art, no matter whether that art was pointedly whole as an Akerman video or scrumbled as a spread by Cecily Brown. The second critic said narrative was important. It's true. Narrative is important. All is and all is important, for I don't believe in the redemptive value of unbridled intent or content, or politics, or history, or the gallery, or the *idée*, or in the stock shock of the new, or in

do more to engage the living and working conditions of women in a national/international arena. // Here is what we heard in response: I think women need

Fecche me drynke,
He drank
And drank, and yaf his felawe drynke also,
Men drynken,
This messager drank sadly ale and wyn,
Nay thou shalt drynken of another tonne
Shall savoure wors than ale
For she drank wyn
She drank,
How fairer been thy brestes than is wyn!
Whan I had dronke a draughte of sweete wyn.
As evere moote I drynken wyn or ale,
But first I make a protestacioun
That I am dronke,
That for dronken was al pale
saugh that he was dronke of ale,
Ful pale he was for dronken

---

the sweet embraceable *nous*. I believe that if there is this, there is also that. I believe if it's not one thing it's not another. I believe the self is an uneffaced aesthetic act, and I believe above all else, in making this gilded object.

•

The aesthetic self is not a divining rod to the wellsprung self or the blotter paper of everyone else. I am not I and I am not the other. I am others and I am I. In the doing and undoing and make-over of me, there is neither the excretory birth of a single consciousness, which is the baked story of biography, nor the splintered self of woodcut history. I am a frozen gesture. I am the raw breath on the back of the neck, and the stifled rising sigh. I am refraction, a rose window slatting your sons and daughters, I am *écriture féminine et masculine*, I claim abstraction and realism, time and waste, the screaming whole of the atomized race, I clot the mouth of this double-vaulted god, taking all my partial-birth abortions, and stuffing them right back in.

let us name the baby Angel, and see if it will die
let us name the baby Joy, and hope to make it cry

more money, their own money in their own hands. –Renee Gladman // First is female education; any serious literacy projects around the world that increase

O Januarie, dronken in plesaunce
I wol drynke licour of the vyne,
I am wont to preche, for to wynne.
So dronke he was,
O dronke man,
Ye fare as folk that dronken were of ale.
And for despit he drank ful muchel moore,
Lo, how that dronken Looth, unkyndely
For dronkenesse is
And dronkenesse is eek a foul record
A lecherous thyng is wyn
A likerous mouth moste han a likerous tayl.
Hath wyn bireved me myn eyen sight?
Ye shul have digestyves
Of wormes, er y take youre laxatyves
Of lawriol, centaure, and fumetere
Of herbe yve, growing in oure yeerd, ther mery is

---

    let us name the baby counterfeit, and if it would object
    let us skewer it with wooden pricks, and stick it
    with straight pins. let us unmake our little lamb,
    and praise its smoke perfection.

Is Madame beautiful? Blue may be beautiful, green is often beautiful, red, periodically beautiful. Women are beautiful. Beauty is beautiful. The arguments between as-is and to-be are foreskinned and foreshadowed. The better aesthetic argument swears not by the testicular tooth of a single truth, even that singular truth of multiplicity, but to the constant tension between expirations, to the thievish shuttering of subject and object, that, like the lead-lined mirror and the serpentine self, is both word for world and word for word and the chiaroscuro in the machine. The purpose of engaging in complimentary constraints is to incant the movement within the raft of the Medusa, enacting the hinge of articulation and swearing by the fact of metamorphosis—so that the less of we, the more of we, for we is the we that we can see, and we's all about eye'd eternity, and the happiness of hope.

female access to education at all levels should be support. Second, people need access to the means of dissemination—books, journals, and libraries, but even

Pekke hem up right as they grow, and ete heme yn!
Til wel ny the day bigan to sprynge.
Here is ended the Host Tale.

When Mother was dying, we lied and said it was all right.

•

What. That. You think so. There is a reason. You think so. What. Nothing. Not that. Not that again. Again, again. No. It is time. No. It is time. No. It is time. No. Not yet. Later. When. Later. How will I know. You will know later. Yes. Now. Yes. Now. No. It isn't time. Now. No. Now. No. Is it time. No. There's no reason. Not yet. Is it true. Yes, it is true. Is it good. Yes, it is good. Is it likely. Yes, it is likely. Is it time. No. When. Later. When. When it is time. Now. No. When. Later. When is later. When it is time. It is time, then. Yes. How do you know. Know what. Know when. When. When it is later. It is time. Then. Not now. Later. When. Yes. When. Yes. When I cannot when we become when there is an unbearable when there is no one left who is not when we are when we understand when we tear off the lash and the lid and rotate our bald eye inward when we are understood when we are we and when we can become when we will understand when we will then when we will. When. When it is not my fault.

more notably now, the internet. Third, U.S. citizens and other first world citizens need to develop a respect for the cultural work accomplished in conditions and

mOUther pOEmes
Christine Wertheim

with traditions and language choices that differ notably from what we know or are comfortable with. –Rachel Blau DuPlessis // I'm interested in the idea of

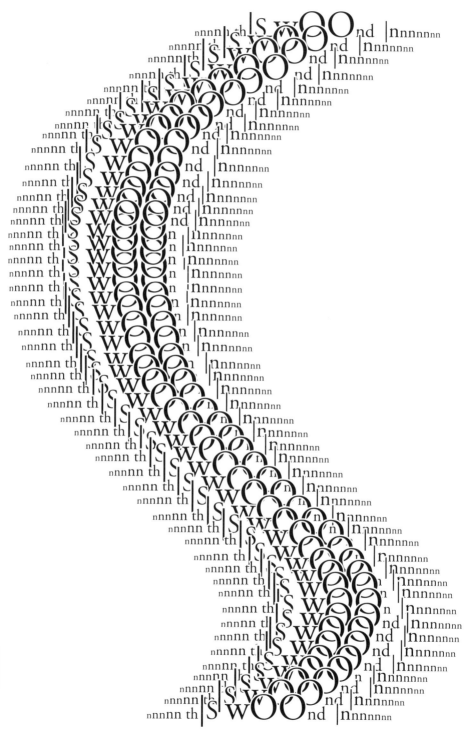

pragmatically hybrid poetry communities: formed to address urgent socio-political matters impacting women. –Joan Retallack // It might continue the

the dirrrrt

|'m so +|red, |'m so +|red, |'m so very very +|red.
did U know, did U know, that the rocks live in the dirt?
+ the girl, she was passing, she was passing,
she was passing by a rock.

+ the rock, it had a mOUth, it had a mOUther full of tEEth.
+ it was living, it was living, it was living in the dirt,

with its tEEth there, with its tEEth there, with its tEEth,
they're in the dirt.
|+ was her mOUth, |+ was her mOUther,
+ |+ was living in the dirt.
+ she was +|red, she was +|red,
she was very very +|red,
with the rock that was her mOUth,

that had some tEEth, there by the road, they're in the dirt,
where she was passing, by the road,
they're in the dirt, there with her mOUth
there with her mOUth, her they're,

there was a longing, there were her tEEth
as she was passing, by a rock, there in the dirt.
They're in the dirt, they're in her mOUth
they're in her moOUther

they are her tEEth, they're in her mOUth, her
they are her mOUth, hers,
they are herrrr mOUther, + they are dirt.
they are herrrr dirrrt
they are herrrr dirrrrt
they arrrr herrrs
they arrrrr herrr,
they arrrr
rrrrrrrr

project of reconstituting awareness of the body as a political site, as matrix and vortex of political halts and flows. –Jennifer Scappettone // I don't know.

ha ha ha ha ha ha ha ha ha ha

ha ha ha ha ha ha ha ha ha ha
++++++++++++++++++++++++
+u+ +u+ +u+ +u+ +u+ +u+ +u+ +u+
               ha ha ha ha ha ha ha ha ha ha
++++++++++++++++++++++++
++++++++++++++++++++++++++++
eeeeeeeeeeeeeheheheheheheheheheheh
       +u+ +u+ +u+ +u+ +u+ +u+ +u+ +u+
heeeheeeeheeeeheeeehehehehehe
++++++++++++++++++++++++++++
uuuuuuuuuuuuurrrrrrrrrrrrr
       eeeeeeeeeeeeeheheheheheheheheheheh
huuuuuh!
      heeeheeeeheeeeheeeehehehehehe
hummmmm h|mmmmen
       uuuuuuuuuuuuurrrrrrrrrrrrr
h|mmmmmen hummmm ha ha ha ha ha ha ha ha
             huuuuuh!
a hum to a h|mn ++++++++++++++++++++++++++
        hummmmm h|mmmmen
   or +u+ +u+ +u+ +u+ +u+ +u+ +u+ +u+
     h|mmmmmen hummmm
a h|men to a hum? ++++++++++++++++++++++++++
     a hum to a h|mn
hmmmmmeeeeeeeeeeeeeheheheheheheheheheheh
       or
     heeeheeeeheeeeheeeehehehehehe
   a h|men to a hum?
   uuuuuuuuuuuuurrrrrrrrrrrrr
hmmmmm?
       huuuuuh!
     hummmmm h|mmmmen
    h|mmmmmen hummmm
      a hum to a h|mn
         or
     a h|men to a hum?
       hmmmmm?

Sometimes I just want to leave my job and do some more direct political work.
–Elizabeth Treadwell // […] but my question goes back to power—who has the

the e|e's a s|te

mmmmmmmm
+he e|e +|s a s|te but +he vO|dse |+'s a 'S-mOuther|n'
so her mouth was re mOved from her pictures
her vO|dse was re mOved from her pictures
her mouth |+ was re mOved her vO|dse |+ was re mOved
her mouth, her mOUth was remOved
her vO|dce was removed
her mouth, her mouth, |+ was ( )
|+ was her mOUth, hers, |+ was hers
|+ was her mOUth
|+ was a S-mOUther|n'
|+ was her mOUth
|+ was her mOUth-hers
|+ was her mOuther
|+ was her mOther
+ |+ was removed.

| o u | o u | o u   a vo|dse   a vo|dse 'n
         e|e 'S plutter   'n | e|e 'S tutter   'n   e|e
mutter |n' m e|e tongue   'n   m e|e 'S   'n   e|e 'S catter
    'n   th e|e 'S plater,   'n   m e|e patter   e|e'S
              th|S woon |n'   th|S woound 'n   the |'S ound
                |n'   the |'S   mother |n'
                  themothers   'n   the mouth here
       |'S the mouth   here ? |'S the mouth   hers ?
              |'S the |'Smother |'S the |'S moUth her?
                |'S the |'S mothere |n'
           the moOth   or in her tears ?
  'n her tears   're   'n her splutter   'n the stutter |n'
         her tongue   'n the scatter   'n the splatter
  'n the th|S woon |n' 'n th|S woound 'n the |'S ound
|n' the |'S mother |n' th|'S mother |n' her tears 'n her
       tears.   how she tEArs . how she tEArs   how she
           tEArs how she tEArs   how she tEArs |n
       me|e tongue 'n   e|e stutter , me|e   'S mutter
                 may e|e mutter'S U a vo|dse?

power to imagine these transforming things, the things that will transform the circumstances or conditions of others? I think it takes a visionary character.

But then, there is the question of confidence. And my thoughts go back to the question of race. –Bhanu Kapil

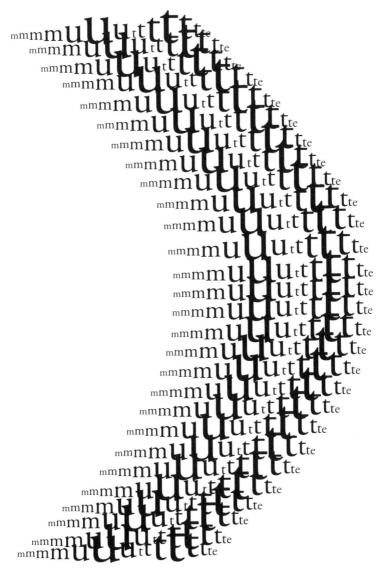

Contributors' Notes

Dodie Bellamy's essays and reviews have appeared in *The Village Voice, The San Francisco Chronicle, Bookforum, Out/Look, Nest,* and *The San Diego Reader* as well as numerous literary journals and web sites. She has also written *Real* (Talisman House, 1994), *The Letters of Mina Harker* (University of Wisconsin Press, 2004), *Pink Steam* (Suspect Thoughts, 2004), *Academonia* (Krupskaya, 2006) and *Barf Manifesto* (Ugly Duckling Presse, 2009). Her book *Cunt-Ups* (Tender Buttons, 2002) won the 2002 Firecracker Alternative Book Award for Poetry.

Caroline Bergvall is a French-Norwegian writer and artist based in London, working across media, languages, and artforms. Her projects and critical research alternate between poetic books, audio pieces, performance-oriented and installed writing projects. Available books/chapbooks include: *Fig* (Salt Books, 2005), *Cropper* (Torque, 2008), *Plessjør* (H-Press, 2008). A new expanded edition of *Alyson Singes* is forthcoming Spring 2010. Recent presentations: PhonoFemme (Vienna), MukHa Museum (Antwerp), Göteborg Poesi Festival (Sweden), Digital Writing/Tate Modern (London), MOMA (NY). Bergvall is currently an AHRC Fellow in the Creative and Performing Arts. www.carolinebergvall.com

Meiling Cheng is a writer and professor living in Los Angeles and teaching at the University of Southern California. Her first book, *In Other Los Angeleses: Multicentric Performance Art* (2002), explores live artworks made in this edge city. She received a 2008 Guggenheim Fellowship to work on her second book, *Beijing Xingwei: Contemporary Chinese Time-based Art*.

Wanda Coleman: A nominee for poet laureate of California (2005), she was C.O.L.A.'s first literary fellow, Department of Cultural Affairs, Los Angeles, 2003-04, with honors that include the 1999 Lenore Marshall Poetry Prize for *Bathwater Wine*, and finalist in the 2001 National Book Awards for *Mercurochrome*. Her books include the novel *Mambo Hips and Make Believe, The Riot Inside Me: More Trials & Tremors, Jazz & Twelve O'Clock Tales* (Black Sparrow Books) and *Ostinato Vamps* (Pitt Poetry Series).

British-Indian by birth and circumstance, **Bhanu Kapil** teaches writing at Naropa University and Goddard College. Her most recent publication is *Humanimal [a project for future children]* (Kelsey Street Press, 2009).

Chris Kraus is a fiction writer and art critic. Her books include *I Love Dick, Torpor,* and *Video Green: Los Angeles Art and the Triumph of Nothingness.* Her forthcoming novel is *Summer of Hate.*

Susan McCabe is the author of four books, including two critical studies— *Elizabeth Bishop: Her Poetics of Loss* (Penn State University Press, 1994) and *Cinematic Modernism: Modern Poetry and Film* (Cambridge University Press, 2005)—and two poetry volumes, *Swirl* (Red Hen Press, 2003), and *Descartes' Nightmare* (winner of the Agha Shahid Ali prize and published by Utah University Press in 2008). She is a professor of English at the University of Southern California.

Tracie Morris is an interdisciplinary poet who has worked extensively as a sound poet and multimedia performer. In addition to her books *Chap-T-her Won: Some Poems* (1993) and *intermission: poems* (2003), her poetry has most recently appeared in *Calalloo, Social* Text, and *Chain* magazines. She has recorded music with composer Elliot Sharp for his group, Terraplane and also works regularly with electronic artist Val Jeanty, among other esteemed artists. Tracie is the recipient of numerous awards for poetry and performance; she holds an MFA from Hunter College, and a PhD from New York University.

Eileen Myles, named by *BUST* magazine "the rock star of modern poetry," is the author of more than twenty books of poetry and prose, including *The Importance of Being Iceland, Chelsea Girls, Cool for You, Sorry, Tree,* and *Not Me*. Myles was head of the writing program at University of California, San Diego, from 2002 to 2007, and she has written extensively on art and writing and the cultural scene. Most recently, she received a Arts Writer grant from the Creative Capital/ Andy Warhol Foundation.

Maggie Nelson is the author of several books including *The Red Parts: A Memoir* (Free Press, 2007), *Women, the New York School, and Other True Abstractions* (University of Iowa Press, 2007), *Something Bright, Then Holes* (Soft Skull Press, 2007), and *Jane: A Murder* (Soft Skull Press, 2005), finalist, the PEN/Martha Albrand Award for the Art of the Memoir. She currently teaches in the School of Critical Studies at Cal Arts and lives in Los Angeles. She is a recipient of an Arts Writers grant from Creative Capital/Andy Warhol Foundation.

Vanessa Place is a writer, lawyer, and co-director of Les Figues Press.

Juliana Spahr is a poet, teacher, and scholar. Her most books include *The Transformation* (Atelos Press, 2007), *This Connection of Everyone with Lungs* (University of California Press, 2005), and *Fuck You-Aloha-I Love You* (Wesleyan University Press, 2001).

Christine Wertheim is MFA Writing Program Chair at Cal Arts. She is the author of +|*'me'S-pace* (Les Figues Press), a book of poetics, and a chapbook from Triage. She co-edited the anthologies *Seancé, Noulipo,* and *Feminaissance. Untitled* is forthcoming. Recent critical work has appeared in *X-tra, Cabinet* and *The Quick and the Dead, Walker Art Centre*. Recent poetry appears in *Drunken Boat, Tarpaulin Sky* and *Veer*. Her new book is a poetic suite on mothers.

Stephanie Young lives and works in Oakland. She edited the anthology *Bay Poetics* (Faux Press, 2006) and is currently at work on the collaborative website *Deep Oakland*. Her books of poetry are *Picture Palace* and *Telling the Future Off*.

Lidia Yuknavitch is the author of several books including *Liberty's Excess* (FC2, 2000), *Allegories of Violence* (Routledge, 2000), and *Real to Reel* (FC2, 2007). Her writing has appeared in several journals, including *Postmodern Culture, Fiction International, Another Chicago Magazine, Zyzzyva, Critical Matrix,* and *Other Voices,* and in the anthologies *Representing Bisexualities* (NYU Press) and *Third Wave Agenda* (University of Minnesota Press). She teaches fiction writing and literature in Oregon.

Acknowledgements

The editor would like to thank the following: The Annenberg Foundation for their generous support of the conference from which this book arose. Nancy Wood, the Dean of Critical Studies at Cal Arts, and all the faculty and staff of the Cal Arts MFA Writing Program. To all the conference participants, including Janet Sarbanes and Yxta Maya Murray and our panel moderators: Anna Joy Springer, Karla Diaz, Janice Lee and Teresa Carmody. Our intern Janice Lee, the Cal Arts MFA Writing students of 2007, and Suzanne Isken and all the staff at MOCA LA who helped make the conference possible. Carol Stakenas at Los Angeles Contemporary Exhibitions. The publishers, Teresa Carmody and Vanessa Place of Les Figues Press, for their gracious support of this book, and to the amazing Les Figues interns, Sophia Kang and Erin Bower, and proofreaders: Harold Abramowitz, Johanna Blakley, Laura Vena and Janice Lee (again). Lastly, Matias Viegener, who taught me how to read.

The essay referred to in the editor's introduction is: Stefania Pandolfo. "The Thin Line of Modernity: Some Moroccan Debates on Subjectivity." *Questions of Modernity*, ed. Timothy Mitchell. Minneapolis London: University of Minnesota Press, 2000. 115-147.

All creative works printed with permission from the authors. Dodie Bellamy, "Sexspace," from *Academonia* (San Francisco: Krupskaya, 2006); Caroline Bergvall, "Points of Pressure," also in *How2*, summer 2009, http://www.asu.edu/pipercwcenter/how2journal/; Wanda Coleman, "RAPE," from *Wanda Coleman's Greatest Hits: 1966-2003*, Series #13, (Columbus, Ohio: Pudding House Publications, 1983, 2004); Bhanu Kapil, from *Incubation: a space for monsters* (New York: Leon Works, 2006); Susan McCabe, from *Swirl* (Los Angeles: Red Hen Press, 2003); Tracie Morris, "Untitled," *Callaloo*, Vol. 25, no. 1, Winter 2002; Eileen Myles, "tapestry," *Vice*, Fiction Issue, 2006, www.viceland.com; Maggie Nelson, excerpts from *The Red Parts* (New York: Free Press, 2007); Juliana Spahr, "Gender Trouble," earlier version in *Boog Reader #8*; Stephanie Young, "Chapter Seven, or, I Do What I Don't Want To Do," from *Picture Palace* (in girum imus nocte et consumimur igni, 2008), and previously in *War and Peace* vol. 3.; Lidia Yuknavitch, "Daguerreotype of a Girl," in *Wreckage of Reason: An Anthology of Contemporary Xxperimental prose by Women Writers*, ed. Nava Renek (Spuyten Duyvil, 2008).

LES FIGUES PRESS
Post Office Box 7736
Los Angeles, CA 90007
www.lesfigues.com
www.lesfigues.blogspot.com